PERIOD MAKE-UP
FOR STUDIO, STAGE & SCREEN

PERIOD MAKE-UP
FOR STUDIO, STAGE & SCREEN

A PRACTICAL REFERENCE FOR ACTORS, MODELS, MAKE-UP ARTISTS, PHOTOGRAPHERS, STAGE MANAGERS & DIRECTORS

Kit Spencer

methuen | drama

A QUINTET BOOK
Copyright © 2008 Quintet Publishing Limited.

This edition published by
Methuen Drama
A & C Black Publishers Ltd
36 Soho Square
London W1D 3QY
www.methuendrama.com

ISBN-13: 978-1-4081-1043-0

QTT.PMU

Conceived, designed, and produced by
Quintet Publishing Limited
The Old Brewery
6 Blundell Street
London N7 9BH

Stylist and Makeup Artist: Kit Spencer
Photographer: Martin Norris
Picture research: Angela Levin, Kobal Collection
Designer: Ian Ascott
Art Editor: Michael Charles
Project Editor: Asha Savjani
Assistant Editor: Robert Davies
Proofreader: Rachel Connolly
Indexer: Vicki Robinson
Managing Editor: Donna Gregory
Publisher: James Tavendale

10 9 8 7 6 5 4 3 2 1

Printed in China by 1010 P   Limited

CONTENTS

Foreword

This fascinating book, by one of today's most talented make-up artists and hairstylists, will appeal not only to the professional make-up artist, actor, director or historian, but to anyone who has ever watched a movie or a play and wanted to know more about the craft of creating the illusions that either enchant or horrify us in the darkened theater. Nowadays there is an incredible range of products and techniques available for the make-up professional, from the subtlety of airbrushing to amazingly life-like animatronics and prosthetics. We can also be fairly certain (we hope!) that our make-up isn't going to kill us, but that wasn't always the case. How did people achieve the glamour or the disguise they wanted, without access to all the new wonders?

This is a great reference guide for actors and directors who want the facts and truths about the "real" make-up, not the dressed-up fake make-up that some movies use and that can ruin the authenticity of a story.

After sixteen years as a professional makeup artist, working primarily in London, Los Angeles and New York, I haven't lost any of my passion for the ancient art of altering (for better or worse) the human face.

Kit Spencer writes in a natural, direct way, entertaining us as well as giving the facts. Her detailed research is certainly informative, but it's also fun to read. Like the best history teachers, she shares her knowledge with an infectious enthusiasm. From the origin of make-up and its uses throughout history, the eternal quest for enhancement by both women and men and the oftentimes poisonous ingredients that killed so many in the process, to the method and application of period theatrical make-up, Ms Spencer's lively narrative will keep you turning pages.

I would highly recommend this book as a teaching manual for make-up for movies, TV and theatre. The steps are easy to follow and the material covered is as extensive as one would expect to find in a top professional make-up school, including related aspects of the film and theatre industry.

Whether you're a seasoned professional, or a curious beginner, whether you apply make-up to others or whether you just wear it yourself, here's a book that you'll refer to for years. So make yourself comfortable and enjoy!

Dani Weiser trained and studied make-up in France and London. She lectured and demonstrated theatrical/ special effects make-up at the Covent Garden Theatre Museum and taught in Los Angeles and New York. Her work includes TV commercials, fashion, movies, advertising and documentaries. She currently resides in New York. Her website is: hollywoodmakeupartist.net

🔘 How to use this book

This book is divided into three sections: Equipment and Techniques, The Gallery and Looks.

EQUIPMENT AND TECHNIQUES

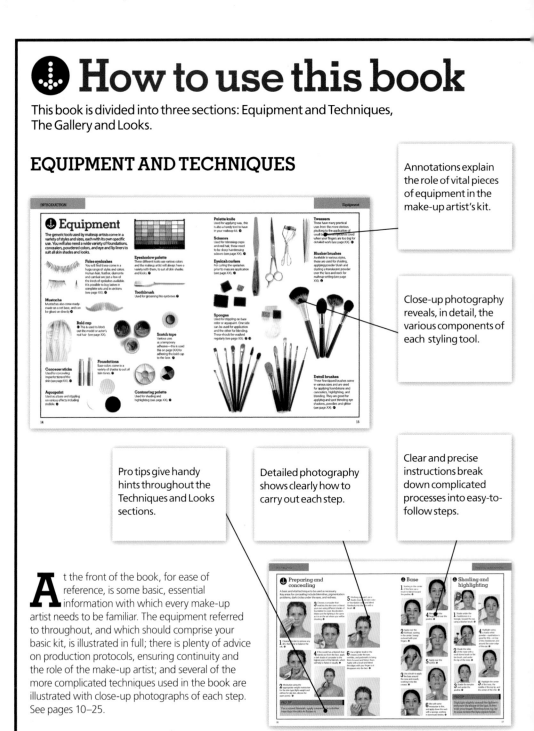

Annotations explain the role of vital pieces of equipment in the make-up artist's kit.

Close-up photography reveals, in detail, the various components of each styling tool.

Pro tips give handy hints throughout the Techniques and Looks sections.

Detailed photography shows clearly how to carry out each step.

Clear and precise instructions break down complicated processes into easy-to-follow steps.

At the front of the book, for ease of reference, is some basic, essential information with which every make-up artist needs to be familiar. The equipment referred to throughout, and which should comprise your basic kit, is illustrated in full; there is plenty of advice on production protocols, ensuring continuity and the role of the make-up artist; and several of the more complicated techniques used in the book are illustrated with close-up photographs of each step. See pages 10–25.

THE GALLERY

From Hollywood movies to fringe theatre, the worlds of studio, stage and screen are fascinated with period productions. The drama and romance of historic settings have made for some memorable productions, which have often tested the shows' make-up artists to their limits. The art of period styling is showcased in this section, with images of iconic styles – mainly modelled by actors performing in movies set in the more distant past – as well as original photographs of classic looks from recent history. This gallery of period looks, both original and recreated, is the inspiration for the next section. See pages 26–53.

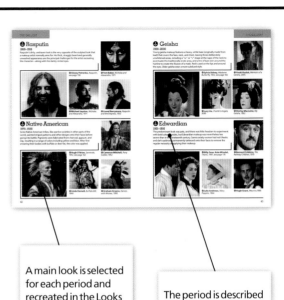

A main look is selected for each period and recreated in the Looks section.

The period is described in terms of tastes and trends in make-up, as well as social and cultural influences.

A list of any equipment you will need, in addition to the main elements of the make-up artist's kit bag.

The main look from the Gallery is blown up full-page for the reader to see exactly what is being recreated.

LOOKS

This is the main body of the book: step-by-step instructions, accompanied by detailed photographs, showing you how to recreate fifty period looks. In each case, inspiration is drawn from one of the images featured in this section. The text is accompanied by pro tips, which introduce you to the secrets of the professional artist – providing hints and information that will make life on set immeasurably easier. Each look lists the key equipment that you will need in addition to the key materials in every artist's kit bag. For some very old looks, pottery and carvings are probably the only pictorial reference points available to make-up artists today. See pages 54–253.

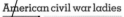

Introduction

There are various elements at play on set and backstage with which the experienced make-up artist will have developed their own routine. Although every set will be run slightly differently, some basic, transferable guidelines are outlined below.

Production protocols and paperwork

Within a production company you will have an Executive Producer, Series Producer, Producer, Production Manager and Production Co-ordinator. Director, Lighting, Make-up and Camera Operators are classified as crew and are hired on a freelance basis. The Line Producer or Production Manager is, therefore, the initial point of contact for the production and is responsible for hiring and firing. They will contact you to check your availability for the shooting dates, negotiate rates and

finalize the terms of your contract. Once you have been confirmed on the job you will be asked to submit an estimated budget for the make-up department, including materials and staff.

If you are working on a drama or film you will initially be sent a schedule, script and the actors' pictures and details from the production office. The person responsible for continuity will provide you with a scene breakdown.

For all types of production, contact details will be exchanged with the Production Co-ordinator who will, prior to the production, send everyone a comprehensive contact list and provide call sheets for each day of the production once filming has begun.

The call sheet is your guide for each day of filming. It will contain the times you need to be present on set, the location of the shoot and contact details of all those involved, as well as notes on health and safety. Before the production starts, you will be asked for your input to estimate the time it will take for each person in make-up. These times will be worked into the overall timeline for the day and included in the call sheet.

Script breakdown, shooting schedules and continuity

Once you have received the script you will need to break it down into the characters, days and then scenes. Using continuity sheets, you need to begin to develop a filing system for the make-up department, perhaps having one file containing the character sheets in alphabetical order and one file divided into shooting days and scenes containing a duplicate of the sheets for each character in those scenes.

You will then need to meet with the Director and Costume Designer to discuss the looks for each character. They will already have an idea of how they would like each character to look but will be keen to have your input and hear any ideas you may have. The Costume Designer will have prepared mood boards for each character and you will be able to reference them when designing the make-up. Once you have been given pictures of the actors, file them with the relevant continuity sheets and make notes of your initial ideas. It is then advisable to talk to the actors themselves to get their input on how they feel their character should look. If the schedule allows, it is advisable to meet with the actors to do a make-up test – this will allow any difficulties or differences of opinion to be ironed out before shooting begins. It will also allow you to better estimate make-up time required and ensure you don't overrun on the first day. Once the make-up has been decided, take a picture of the actor and attach it to the continuity sheet.

Before shooting begins, you should create and label a make-up bag for each character. This should contain the make-up or styling products required to create their agreed look. These can then be passed, along with the continuity

sheets, to anyone in the make-up department working with that particular character so they can create the required look.

When shooting begins, a picture should be taken of each actor in each scene and placed in the relevant place in the continuity folder.

Safety and sanitation on set

The call sheet will outline the safety details for each day, highlighting any specific safety issues at the location. If you're shooting outdoors, the expected weather conditions will be

outlined and you should ensure you dress appropriately. When on set, common sense should prevail. There will be lots of cables, kit boxes, overhead lights and moving cameras.

You should ensure all your electrical items are working correctly and are safety tested regularly.

Synthetic make-up brushes used for bases, concealers and lipsticks and glosses should be cleaned with brush cleaner after each face you use them on. This will stop product and bacteria build up.

You should keep a separate lip brush and powder puff in your set bag for each person. Brushes used with powder products should be wiped clean with a dry tissue after

every use and washed with a mild detergent at the end of each day.

It is very easy to pass on contaminations through mascara. For this reason, you should use disposable wands, which are available from professional make-up suppliers.

Before you start make-up on someone you should ask them if they have any known allergies to particular products.

Purchasing for production

Once you know the make-up requirements for each character, you can begin to estimate the costs involved. You will have been given a guideline of the available budget – taking this into account along with

the make-up requirements will give you an idea of what is affordable. You will then be able to begin to make purchasing decisions and decide how best to spend your budget.

Designing a look

Before you start make-up, while you are introducing yourself to the model or actor, make a visual assessment of their face and eye shape, skin tone and condition. Begin to make product choices in your head based on what you see, and start to consider what make-up would suit them.

The first make-up step should always be to prepare the skin. This has a dual purpose: firstly to clean the skin and balance the oil

production, and secondly so you can feel the texture of the skin and structure of the bones beneath the surface. With practice you will instantly know what products are going to work best and what make-up would best suit their face. Make-up for the stage is much more exaggerated, as it needs to make an impact from a distance.

⚙ Equipment

The generic tools used by make-up artists come in a variety of styles and sizes, each with its own specific use. You will also need a wide variety of foundations, concealers, powdered colours and eye and lip liners to suit all skin shades and looks.

False eyelashes
You will find these come in a huge range of styles and colours. Human hair, feather, diamante and carnival are just a few of the kinds of eyelashes available. It is possible to buy lashes in complete sets and in sections (see page 22). ⊖

Eyeshadow palette
These different looks use various colours and the make-up artist will always have a selection with them, to suit all skin shades and looks. ➊

Toothbrush
Used for grooming the eyebrows. ➊

Moustache
Moustaches also come ready-made on a net base, and can be glued on directly. ➋

Bald cap
⊖ This is used to block out the model or actor's real hair (see page 162).

Scotch tape
Various uses as a temporary adhesive – this is used on page 162 for adhering the bald cap to the face. ➊

Foundations
Base colours come in a variety of shades and textures to suit all skin tones. ➊

Stick foundation
Used for a heavier base – a modern version of the pan stick. ➋

Aquapaint
Used as a base and for stippling on various effects including stubble. ➋

Concealing wheel
Used for concealing imperfections. ➊

Contouring palette
Used for shading and highlighting (see page 17). ➊

Palette knife

Used for applying wax, this is also a handy tool to have in your make-up kit. ➡

Scissors

Used for trimming crepe and real hair, these need to be sharp hairdressing scissors (see page 24). ➡

Eyelash curlers

For curling the eyelashes prior to mascara application (see page 23). ➡

Sponges

Used for stippling on base colour or aquapaint. One side can be used for application and the other for blending. Wash after every use. ⬆ + ➡

Tweezers

These have many practical uses from the more obvious plucking to the application of small bunches of eyelashes. Used when your fingers are too big for detailed work (see page 22). ⬅

Make-up brushes

Available in various styles, these are used for shading, detail work, applying powder blush and dusting a translucent powder over the face and neck for make-up setting (see page 17). Finer-tipped brushes come in various sizes and are used for applying foundations and concealers, highlighting and blending. They are good for applying and spot blending eye shadows, powders and glitter. ⬅

Preparing and concealing

A basic and vital technique to be used as necessary. Key areas for concealing include blemishes, pigmentation problems, dark circles under the eyes and redness.

1 Cleanse the skin to remove any dirt, then tone to balance the oils. ⬆

2 Moisturize using the appropriate weight moisturiser for the skin type (lightweight and oil-free for oily skin; silicone for open pores). ⬆

3 Choose a concealer that matches the skin tone or blend your own using different shades of foundation to cover discolouration. Make sure the lighting is the same as it is on the set where you will be shooting. ⬇

4 If the model has a blemish that stands out from the face, apply a dark shade of concealer to the highest point of the blemish, which will help to flatten it visually. ⬇

5 Working outwards, use a shade close to the skin colour or foundation colour and blend flawlessly into the skin with a brush. ⬇

6 Use a lighter shade in the creases under the eyes, wrinkles and pockmarks to bring them forwards and flatten them. Apply with a brush and blend the edges with your finger so it disappears into the face. ⬇

PRO TIP

For a raised blemish, apply concealer in a darker tone than the skin to flatten it.

🔅 Base

1 Starting in the centre of the face use a brush to blend towards the jawline. ⬇

2 Apply over the forehead, starting in the centre. Sweep outwards with your fingers. ⬇

3 Use a brush to apply the base around the nose and mouth, working it into the creases. ⬇

4 Blend with the fingers and over the jawline. ⬆

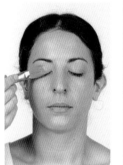

5 Apply over the eyelids. ⬆

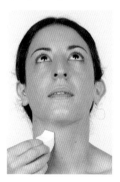

6 Mix with some moisturiser to thin, and apply down the neck with a sponge, working in downwards strokes. ⬆

🔅 Shading and highlighting

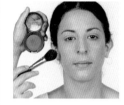

1 Shade under the cheekbones in a triangle towards the ear with a blusher brush. ⬆

2 Shade the sides of the nose with a small dome brush or flat fan brush, and under the tip of the nose. ⬆

3 Shade the temples and under the jawline. ⬆

4 Highlight using a matt white powder – eyeshadow is good for this – on top of the cheekbones and around the outer edge of the eye. ⬆

5 Highlight the centre of the nose, the middle of the top lip and the centre of the chin. ⬆

PRO TIP

Highlight slightly around the lipline to enhance their shape. Soften with your finger. Shading from the top lip to the nose makes the lips appear fuller.

⚉ Straight make-up for men

This basic technique applies to all looks and styles – vary the shade, consistency or texture to suit the look you are going to recreate.

1 Apply a light wash of base, preferably a cream cake base. Alternatively you can use aquacolour with a wet sponge, but once you have started to apply it to the skin you need to work fast as the water evaporates quickly. ➲

2 With a colour slightly lighter than the base colour, highlight the high point of the eyelid. Feel for the middle of the eyeball through the skin. ⊙

3 Cover any blemishes and shadows around the eyes. Add a lighter colour into any pitted scars and a dark colour on the top of any raised scars. Apply concealer with a synthetic concealer brush and then lightly tap with your finger around the edges to blend into the skin. ➲

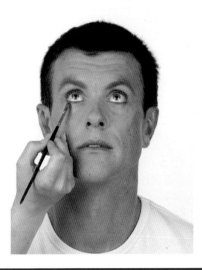

4 Set base with loose translucent powder; press into the skin until it disappears with a velour puff. ⬆

🌢 Hiding beard shadow

A straightforward concealing technique that is often necessary when working on set all day.

1 Apply aquacolour using a wet sponge, working quickly before it dries. ⬆

3 Blend the edges in with your finger. ⬇

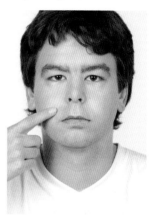

5 For a natural, healthy look, add a small amount of a natural matt peach blusher on either side of the nose in an upside down triangular shape. ⬆

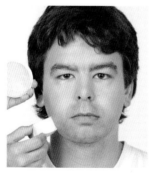

2 Apply the colour, covering the chosen area thoroughly and using the dry side of the sponge to work the colour into the skin. ⬆

4 Powder to set using a velour puff. ⬆

PRO TIP

If more cover is required, add a small amount of red greasepaint or lipstick in dots over the beard area, then blend base over the top.

Lip shapes

Different looks use different lip shapes, so it will be necessary to alter your model's natural lip shape.

Normal

1 Pencil in the centre of the top lip first, working towards the middle from one side at a time. ⬆

3 Pencil in the centre of the bottom lip. ⬆

2 Press above the lip with your thumb to plump the lip, and draw from the outsides in. ⬆

4 Plump the lip with your thumb and draw from the outside in, one side at a time, and go back over in both directions so the line doesn't break. ⬆

Bow

1 Starting at the top, one side at a time, draw half a circle inside the natural lip line from the outside towards the middle. Match the other side to this, standing back as you work to make sure the sides are equal. ⬇

2 Draw inwards a bit at a time from each side. ⬇

3 Start in the middle of the bottom lip and draw outwards a bit at a time. ⬇

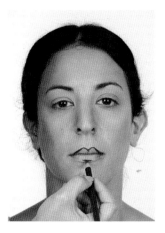

Full

1 Outline a cupid's bow just outside the natural lipline. ⬇

3 Draw in the middle of the bottom lip just outside the natural lip line. ⬆

2 From the outside in, join the edges of the top lip up to the cupid's bow. ⬇

4 These lips are smaller than normal lips so you will need to decide on the point at which they should finish, and mark this with a dot on both sides before filling the lines, one side at a time, by drawing in from the dots. ⬆

4 Draw from the outside edges to join in the middle. ⬆

PRO TIP

Rest your hand on a velour puff to steady it. Fill in with a pencil to create a long-lasting base.

⚙ False eyelashes

Changing fashions have meant that eyelash shapes have varied throughout history.

Individual

1 Select the size required (smaller lashes go towards the middle of the lash line). ⬇

2 Apply a dab of glue to the end of one lash bunch and wait for it to go tacky. ⬇

3 Attach using tweezers – hold the lashes, angling them so they mimic the shape of the natural lashes. ⬇

4 Press into the roots of the lashes. ⬆

5 Repeat, with longer lashes towards the outside of the lash line. ⬆

6 Lightly mascara over lashes. ⬆

Full set

1 Measure the width of the false eyelashes against the eye and trim the length if necessary. If the eyelash set is too long, it will be hard to apply and you will end up sticking top and bottom together. ⬇

2 Glue along the seam and wait for the glue to go tacky. ⬇

3 With the help of tweezers, place the lashes at the roots of the model's own lashes, pressing them into place. ⬆

4 When the glue is dry, apply mascara (see page 23). ⬆

PRO TIP

When gluing false lashes, curling natural lashes or applying mascara, use the thumb of one hand to raise the eyebrow and make the skin taut.

❶ Curling eyelashes

Eyelash curlers are used to open up the eyes before applying mascara.

1 Ask the model to look down. ⬇

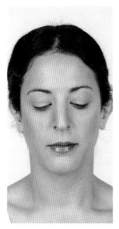

2 With the model looking down, lift the eyebrow. ⬇

3 Close the eyelash curler over the roots of the eyelashes and squeeze the hairs. ⬆

4 Release the curlers. ⬆

PRO TIP

Changing the direction of the mascara wand when applying will mean that all surfaces of the eyelash are coated in mascara, increasing volume.

❷ Applying mascara

Used to define the eyelashes and increase volume and length.

1 Ask the model to look at the floor. ⬇

2 Lift the eyebrow. ⬇

3 Sweep the brush vertically through the top lashes. ⬇

4 Sweep the brush horizontally up from the roots. ⬆

5 Vertically sweep outwards through the corner lashes. ⬆

6 Pick out individual lashes vertically on the bottom eyelid. ⬆

⚙ Preparing facial hair

This straightforward technique uses crepe hair, for application with spirit gum as a beard, moustache or sideburns (see page 25).

3 Iron the hair with a steam iron until the wave has gone out of it. Stretch it out by gently pulling the ends away from each other. ⬇

1 Pull strands of hair off the cords they are folded onto. ⬆

4 Comb through so that any loose hairs are removed. This is the same as drawing through a hackle. ⬇

5 Repeat with another colour (match to model's own hair colour) for blending. ⬆

2 Cut slightly longer than the length of hair desired. ⬆

PRO TIP

Don't throw away any waste hair – save it to use in hair pads made from a hair net.

6 Blend the two shades of hair into each other by rolling them between your fingers. ⬆

⚛ Applying a moustache

Moustaches come in a variety of shades and sizes, lengths and styles – they are all applied using this same basic technique.

1 Iron some crepe hair and prepare for facial use, mixing the hair to match the model's own colouring (see page 24). ⬇

2 Outline the desired final shape of the moustache onto the face using a very light eyebrow pencil. ⬇

3 Paint a thin layer of spirit gum along the outside of the marked moustache area, one side at a time. ⬇

4 Gather a small bunch of prepared crepe hair between the middle and forefinger of your laying hand (i.e. the right hand if you are right handed or the left hand if you are left handed). Fan the hair out by rolling between your fingers. ⬆

5 Push the hairs into the glue line, angling them so that just the tips are glued to give a more natural-lying result. Press the hairs firmly into the glue. ⬇

6 Roll over the hair with a pencil or the handle of a brush to secure the hair against the glue. ⬆

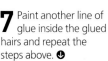

7 Paint another line of glue inside the glued hairs and repeat the steps above. ⬇

8 Repeat again. When all hair has been laid, wait for a few minutes and place a clean towel over the moustache, pressing firmly, and hold it there for 30 seconds. ⬇

9 When you have finished laying the hair, gently pull out any loose hairs to thin the moustache, and begin to trim the hairs, taking off a little at a time and assessing before snipping more each time. ⬆

10 Turn the scissors in a vertical direction and trim a little upwards, randomly snipping into the hairs from the middle towards the outer edge for a natural finish. ⬆

PRO TIP

Lay the hairs in a direction that considers the desired shape of the finished moustache.

THE

GALLERY

Introduction

The Gallery section is the red carpet of this book, on which actors and actresses strut their stuff dressed as characters from across the ages. The looks illustrated on these pages have been chosen for authenticity and their faithfulness to the period of history they depict, as well as for their colour and dramatic impact. When recreating period looks, Hollywood has had a tendency, in the past, to come to its own conclusions about how people wore their hair and did their make-up, and different periods have often been misrepresented in film and on television sets because of this. Make-up and dress have been tailored to suit the tastes of modern-day audiences, who would not take to the portrayal of different looks in the same way that contemporary audiences might have done. This is something that make-up artists have to bear in mind when they are asked to recreate a certain look on set. They must be accurate in their representation of the styles from different periods, and they must attempt to be faithful to history. But the make-up artist also has the task of creating a look that will evoke the personality of their character in the mind of their audience. With these various elements at play, a main look has been selected for each of the periods featured in this gallery, and it has been reproduced in clear and comprehensive steps, along with illustrations, in the Looks section on pages 54 to 253.

⚅ Prehistoric

250,000 BCE–3,200 BCE

This look is shaggy and unkempt. Make-up didn't exist in the Stone Age but it is certainly required in order to recreate this look. Crepe hair and stage dirt are a necessity and heavy styling will be required to make your actor or model appear ragged and dirty.

⊕ *Skullduggery*, 1969

⊕ **John Lone,** *Iceman*, 1984, see page 54

⊕ **Robin Williams,** *Being Human*, 1993

⊕ **Everett Mcgill,** *Quest For Fire*, 1981

⚅ Ancient Egypt

3150 BCE–30 BCE

Aristocratic Egyptians could buy products which added a blush to their cheeks and gloss to their lips; but the most frequently used product was a pigment used to add colour and an almond shape to the eyes. Two principal eye colourants were available: *udju*, made from green malachite, and *mesdemet*, a dark grey pigment derived from lead.

⊕ **Gene Tierney, Judith Evelyn,** *The Egyptian*, 1954

⊕ **Elizabeth Taylor,** *Cleopatra*, 1963, see page 58

⊕ **Jack Hawkins,** *Land of the Pharaohs*, 1955

⊕ **Elizabeth Taylor,** *Cleopatra*, 1963

🔅 Ancient Greece

1100 BCE–140 BCE

Most Greek women used cosmetics only very lightly. Sometimes they used white lead to lighten their skin. They could obtain a kind of lipstick made by grinding a pigment with lard. Honey was widely used to moisturise the skin.

⊕ **Diane Kruger,** *Troy*, 2004

⊕ **Angelina Jolie, Val Kilmer, Colin Farrell,** *Alexander*, 2004, see page 62

⊕ **Ursula Andress,** *Clash of The Titans*, 1980

⊕ **Brad Pitt,** *Troy*, 2004

🔅 Ancient Rome

30 BCE–400 CE

Cosmetics were serious business in ancient Rome: upper-class women used lead to whiten their skin, painted their eyelids in subtle shades, rouged their cheeks and lips and used a mixture of butter and barley flour to cure skin blemishes. Pumice stones were rubbed against the teeth to whiten them.

⊕ **Jean Simmons,** *The Robe*, 1953

⊕ **Deborah Kerr,** *Quo Vadis*, 1951, see page 66

⊕ **Joaquin Phoenix,** *Gladiator*, 2000

⊕ **Connie Nielsen,** *Gladiator*, 2000

🜚 Mayan girl

250 CE–900 CE

The ancient Maya painted their faces and bodies regularly. Paint was applied using ceramic slices dipped into the pot of pigment. Tattooing was also practised to adorn the face with patterns and geometric designs. The teeth were filed to exaggerate their pointedness, and the holes were filled with jade.

⊕ *Apocalypto*, 2006, see page 70

⊕ **Dalia Hernandez, Rudy Youngblood,** *Apocalypto,* 2006

⊕ *Apocalypto,* 2006

⊕ *Apocalypto,* 2006

🜚 Eastern warrior

1200 CE–1400 CE

The Mongols – a group of Turkic and Mongolic tribes led to prominence by the great warrior Genghis Khan – were nomadic warriors from the steppes of central Asia. They tended to wear facial hair, which may be either narrow and pointed, or thick and bushy.

⊕ **Yul Brynner,** *Taras Bulba,* 1962, see page 74

⊕ **Tadanobu Asano,** *Mongol,* 2007

⊕ **Patrick Gallagher,** *Night At The Museum,* 2006

⊕ **Zhang Ziyi,** *Musa,* 2005

✪ Celtic warrior

1300–1350

The Celts' success on the battlefield depended partly on the impact of their appearance. For this reason, like many other warrior societies, they wore vivid body paint when fighting. Woad, a pigment made from a plant cultivated across Eurasia, was the key ingredient in Celtic body paint.

⊕ **Mel Gibson,** *Braveheart*, 1995, see page 78

⊕ **Catherine McCormack, Mel Gibson,** *Braveheart*, 1995

⊕ *Braveheart*, 1995

⊕ **Catherine McCormack, Mel Gibson,** *Braveheart*, 1995

✪ Italian Renaissance

1450–1600

The most popular cosmetic product of the age was probably lead paint, worn by many rich women to whiten their face. The toxicity of lead meant that many of these women became gravely ill – and it is believed that some aristocratic husbands died of lead poisoning caused by kissing their wives.

⊕ **Olivia Hussey,** *Romeo and Juliet*, 1968, see page 82

⊕ **Jeremy Irons,** *The Merchant of Venice*, 2004

⊕ **Valentina Cervi,** *Artemisia*, 1997

⊕ **Gabriel Gabrio,** *Lucretia Borgia*, 1935

🌑 Tudor England

1485–1600

Tudor women lavished great care on their appearance, and surviving books on beauty include notes on the use of snail water, cuttlefish bone, eggs, herbs and honey as cosmetic products. Men often had long, thick beards – a style most familiar to us today from paintings of King Henry VIII.

⊕ Keith Michell, *Henry VIII and His Six Wives*, 1972, see page 86

⊕ Natalie Portman, Scarlett Johansson, *The Other Boleyn Girl*, 2008

⊕ Jonathan Timmins, *The Prince and the Pauper*, 2000

⊕ Raquel Welch, *The Prince and the Pauper*, 1977

🌑 Elizabethan England

1560–1600

Pale skin was, for the Elizabethans, a sign of nobility and wealth. Skin problems and pox were rife at this time and skin creams and ointments were out-of-reach for all but the rich. To achieve pale skin, ceruse was used, made from white lead and vinegar. Those who listened to the warnings about lead used a paste of alum and ash or sulphur, or a foundation made using boiled egg white and talcum powder.

⊕ Samantha Morton, *Elizabeth: The Golden Age*, 2007, see page 90

⊕ Clive Owen, *Elizabeth: The Golden Age*, 2007

⊕ Colin Firth, Judi Dench, *Shakespeare in Love*, 1998

⊕ Cate Blanchett, *Elizabeth: The Golden Age*, 2007

 Restoration

1660–1690

It was believed that the body's natural oils protected against disease and so bathing was rare. Scented waters and pomades were therefore popular. There was a preoccupation with having white teeth, but people used gunpowder and acid to achieve this, which in fact made their teeth fall out – it's no surprise that a fashion for speaking with a lisp came into vogue during this period.

Alec Guinness, *Cromwell*, 1970, see page 94

Sir Cedric Hardwicke, *Nell Gwyn*, 1934

Kim Novak, *The Amorous Adventures of Moll Flanders*, 1965

Linda Darnell, *Forever Amber*, 1947

 Gothic

1700–2001

A white face should give the illusion of being very pale. Use a base just one or two shades lighter than your own skin tone, and then put white powder over it for an ethereal, almost greyish cast. Heavy eyes and blood-red lips should be bold but, above all, the key to this look is originality.

Theda Bara, 1917, see page 98

Fairuza Balk, *The Craft*, 1996

Anjelica Huston, *The Addams Family*, 1991

Nicole Kidman, *Birthday Girl*, 2001

⚙ 18th-century France (man)

1700–1800

Elegant gentlemen rouged their cheeks and lips with a rusty colour. Some men took it further and whitened their faces and shaved off their eyebrows – they would then redraw them higher up.

⊕ **John Malkovich,** *Dangerous Liaisons*, 1988, see page 102

⊕ **Dustin Hoffman,** *Perfume: The Story of a Murderer*, 2006

⊕ **Donald Sutherland,** *Fellini's Casanova*, 1976

⊕ **Simon Callow, Greta Scacchi,** *Jefferson In Paris*, 1995

⚙ 18th-century France (woman)

1700–1800

Make-up in this period used natural colours and a pale base combined with a pink, dusky blush and natural eyebrows. A lot of attention was given to jewellery and hair.

⊕ **Lena Olin,** *Casanova*, 2005, see page 106

⊕ **Noemie Godin-Vigneau,** *Nouvelle France*, 2008

⊕ **Glenn Close,** *Dangerous Liaisons*, 1988

⊕ **Mira Sorvino,** *Triumph of Love*, 2001

🌑 Regency England

1715–1835

Ladies of Georgian and Regency England used lead-based white and red paints for their face, which had already been proved deadly. Smaller lips were fashionable, with rouged cheeks and thin, arched eyebrows. Women often wore face patches to cover blemishes or marks.

⊕ Beryl Reid, *Joseph Andrews*, 1976, see page 110

⊕ Rhys Ifans, *Vanity Fair*, 2004

⊕ Matthew Macfadyen, Simon Woods, *Pride and Prejudice*, 2005

⊕ Greer Garson, Laurence Olivier, *Pride and Prejudice*, 1940

🌑 Imperial Russia

1720–1917

The look combines a perfect complexion with pale, matt skin, and sculpted features with heavy brows and defined eyes. Women wore bonnets and used parasols to keep out of the sun, as white skin signified a life of leisure.

⊕ Audrey Hepburn, *War and Peace*, 1956, see page 114

⊕ Alfred Molina, Mia Kirschner, *Anna Karenina*, 1997

⊕ Henry Fonda, *War and Peace*, 1956

⊕ John Gilbert, *The Cossacks*, 1928

 Pirate

1800–1900

A bronzed skin colour, indicative of a life lived outdoors exposed to sun and wind on the high seas, is typical of this look. Brows are heavy and hair is unkempt. Men have a lot of facial hair and both sexes have heavy brows – this is an ungroomed, rough and ready look by all accounts.

Johnny Depp, *Pirates of the Caribbean: Dead Man's Chest*, 2006, see page 118

Dustin Hoffman, *Hook*, 1991

Peter Ustinov, *Blackbeard's Ghost*, 1968

Jean Peters, *Anne of the Indies*, 1951

Wild-west girl

1800–1970

This is a healthy look with a tanned, outdoorsy complexion. The classic, timeless image of the Western cowgirl is of blonde hair in pigtails, a cowboy hat and a checked shirt. Make-up is neutral and subtle, emphasizing the healthy red glow to the cheeks and the slightly bronzed overall complexion.

Jane Fonda, portrait, 1965, see page 122

Doris Day, *Calamity Jane*, 1953

Ella Raines, *Tall In The Saddle*, 1944

Grace Kelly, portrait, 1952

37

⚫ Wild-west man

1800–1970

A rugged, unshaven look, with a tanned and weathered complexion. Sideburns and facial hair play a large part in this make-up, and the make-up artist will need their stubble wax at hand.

⊕ **Dennis Quaid,** *The Alamo,* 2004, see page 126

⊕ **Walter Brennan,** *The Cowboy and the Lady,* 1938

⊕ **Lee Marvin,** *Monte Walsh,* 1970

⊕ **Dermot Mulroney,** *Young Guns,* 1988

⚫ Napoleonic

1805–1815

During the Napoleonic era, women in particular were heavily made up. Cosmetics came from all over, in particular Venice. Ceruse was highly utilized by bourgeois women – a smooth, porcelain complexion was a symbol of refinement, and belladonna was used in the eyes to dilate the pupils.

⊕ **Harvey Keitel,** *The Duellists,* 1977, see page 130

⊕ **John Neville,** *Adventures of Gerard,* 1970

⊕ **Albert Dieudonne,** *Napoleon,* 2003

⊕ **Virginia Mayo,** *Captain Horatio Hornblower,* 1951

19th-century Paris

1830–1900

Until well into the nineteenth century, make-up was thick and greasy, and it was rarely worn by French women, except actresses. Alexandre Napoleon Bourjois, a Parisian perfumier, revolutionized the cosmetics industry by designing make-up of a higher quality – including the world's first powder blusher, released in 1863.

Nicole Kidman, Ewan McGregor, *Moulin Rouge,* 2001, see page 134

Emmanuelle Beart, *Time Regained / Le Temps Retrouve,* 1999

Minnie Driver, *The Phantom of the Opera,* 2004

Vincent Perez, Marie-France Pisier, *Time Regained / Le Temps Retrouve,* 1999

Victorian lady

1840–1900

Paleness – emphasizing one's fragility and delicacy – was the essential look of the period. Few ladies wore heavy make-up, which was associated mainly with thickly powdered actresses like Sarah Bernhardt. In the United States, cosmetic products such as anti-aging creams hit the market in 1886, launched by Harriet Hubbard Ayer's cosmetic company.

Julianne Moore, *An Ideal Husband,* 1998, see page 138

Anna Neagle, *Victoria The Great,* 1937

Norma Shearer, *The Barretts of Wimpole Street,* 1934

Ingrid Bergman, *Gaslight,* 1944

 Poor Victorian

1840–1900

Poor Victorian women used make-up for corrective purposes, rather than to highlight their own features. Coarse cosmetics were available to disguise disease and blemishes. For men and children, the make-up artist should convey an impression of unwashed, undernourished people on the poverty line.

⊕ **Jack Wild,** *Oliver!*, 1968

⊕ **Helena Bonham Carter,** *Sweeney Todd*, 2007, see page 142

⊕ **George C. Scott,** *A Christmas Carol*, 1984

⊕ **Freddie Jones,** *The Elephant Man*, 1980

 Victorian colonial

1840–1900

Short grey hair – often worn slicked back by younger men – and a bristling moustache, were typical of the Victorian colonial male. Formal-looking safari wear was worn with a stiff-collared shirt, cream breeches tucked into brown riding boots, a brown leather belt with a gun holster and a pith helmet.

⊕ **Nigel Green,** *Zulu*, 1963, see page 146

⊕ **Ulla Jacobssen,** *Zulu*, 1963

⊕ **Errol Flynn,** *The Charge of The Light Brigade*, 1936

⊕ **Anna Neagle,** *The Lady with a Lamp*, 1951

US Civil War soldier

1861–1865

Grooming was, needless to say, not a priority. The make-up artist should create a bronzed, weathered look and experiment with stage dirt, stippling on crepe hair over moustache wax. Facial hair can range from stubble to a heavy moustache and unkempt sideburns.

Arthur Hunnicutt, *The Red Badge of Courage*, 1951

Jeff Daniels, *Gettysburg*, 1993, see page 150

Sam Elliott, *Gettysburg*, 1993

Denzel Washington, *Glory*, 1989

US Civil War lady

1861–1865

Few periods are as beloved by moviemakers and dramatists as the American Civil War. This gives the make-up artist the opportunity to experiment with the classic "southern belle" look – exemplified most famously by Vivien Leigh as Scarlett O'Hara in *Gone with the Wind*. This character type is beautiful, hospitable, well-mannered and flirtatious yet chaste; and her make-up should reflect these traits.

Winona Ryder, *Little Women*, 1994

Vivien Leigh, *Gone with the Wind*, 1939, see page 154

Olivia De Havilland, *Gone with the Wind*, 1939

Renee Zellweger, Nicole Kidman, *Cold Mountain*, 2003

 Rasputin

1869–1916

Rasputin's dirty, unshaven look is the very opposite of the sculpted look that a make-up artist normally aims for. His thick, straggly beard and generally unwashed appearance are the principal challenges for the artist recreating this character – along with the darkly circled eyes.

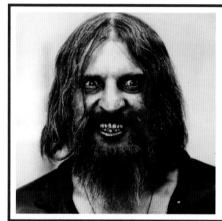

⊕ **Alexey Petrenko,** *Rasputin,* see page 158

⊕ **Michael Jayston,** *Nicholas and Alexandra,* 1971

⊕ **Tom Baker,** *Nicholas and Alexandra,* 1971

⊕ **Lionel Barrymore,** *Rasputin and the Empress,* 1932

 Native American

1870–1930

Some Native American tribes, like warrior societies in other parts of the world, painted striped patterns and other designs onto their faces before going into battle. Pigments were fabricated from charcoal, gypsum and clay, resulting in a range of colours including yellow and blue. After first smearing their bodies with buffalo or deer fat, the colour was applied.

⊕ **Hugh O'Brian,** *Seminole,* 1952, see page 162

⊕ **Cameron Mitchell,** *Pony Soldier,* 1952

⊕ **Linda Darnell,** *Buffalo Bill,* 1944

⊕ **Graham Greene,** *Dances with Wolves,* 1990

⚫ Geisha

1900–2000

Young geisha make-up features a heavy, white base (originally made from lead) that covers the face, neck and chest, leaving three deliberately unwhitened areas, including a "w" or "v" shape at the nape of the neck to accentuate this traditionally erotic area, and a line of bare skin around the hairline to create the illusion of a mask. Red is used on the lips and around the eyes. Older geisha wear a more subdued style.

⊕ **Sylvia Sidney,** *Madame Butterfly,* 1932, see page 166

⊕ **Youki Kudoh,** *Memoirs of a Geisha,* 2005

⊕ **Lucy Liu,** *Charlie's Angels,* 2000

⊕ **Shirley MacLaine,** *My Geisha,* 1962

⚫ Edwardian

1901–1910

The predominant look was pale, and there was little freedom to experiment with bold colours or styles, but Edwardian make-up was nevertheless less severe than in the nineteenth century. Some society women had red cheeks and dark eyebrows permanently tattooed onto their faces to remove the regular necessity of applying their make-up.

⊕ **Billy Zane, Kate Winslet,** *Titanic,* 1997, see page 170

⊕ **Bernard Cribbins,** *The Railway Children,* 1970

⊕ **Julie Andrews,** *Mary Poppins,* 1964

⊕ **Hugh Grant,** *Maurice,* 1988

🌑 America's sweetheart

1913–1950

Mary Pickford's doe-eyed look, with softly lined eyes and pale cheeks, was crucial to her success. As late as 1919 – when she was 27 – Pickford played a young child in a silent movie; and her make-up was crucial to her carefully crafted public image as an American innocent.

⊕ Mary Pickford, portrait, 1917, see page 174

⊕ **Mary Pickford**, portrait

⊕ **Lillian Gish,** portrait

⊕ **Mary Pickford**, portrait

🌑 Jazz-age flapper

1918–1929

The increasingly uninhibited society of the roaring 20s experimented with more daring looks, and more innovative products, than women before the Great War dared to try. The suntanned look, made popular by Coco Chanel, became popular later in the decade; at the same time, Elizabeth Arden began to market cleansing creams to smooth and protect the skin.

⊕ Clara Bow, portrait, 1926, see page 178

⊕ **Betty Balfour**, portrait, 1924

⊕ **Catherine Zeta-Jones,** *Chicago*, 2002

⊕ **Marilyn Monroe,** *Some Like it Hot*, 1959

🌑 Jazz-age socialite

1918–1929

The make-up of mature society women was just as daring as that worn by the younger – and often more controversial – flappers. Women opted for eyeshadow in shades of blue and green, with crimson-coloured lips and a jewelled headdress adding to the overall impression of bright tones and sparkling effects.

⊕ **Gloria Swanson,** portrait, 1928

⊕ **Maggie Smith,** *Quartet*, 1981, see page 182

⊕ **Dianne Wiest,** *Bullets over Broadway*, 1994

⊕ **Kirsten Dunst,** *The Cat's Meow*, 2001

🌑 1930s depression

1929–1939

The down-and-out hobo look relies on a dirtied and dishevelled appearance, usually complemented with a couple of days' stubble growth and, in general, a lightly made-up look. The touchstone film of the period is *The Grapes of Wrath*, based on Steinbeck's novel documenting the troubles of an Oklahoma family.

⊕ **Barbara Pepper, Tom Keene, Karen Morley,** *Our Daily Bread*, 1934

⊕ **William Powell,** *My Man Godfrey*, 1936, see page 186

⊕ **Dorris Bowden, Henry Fonda,** *The Grapes of Wrath*, 1940

⊕ **John Turturro, Tim Blake Nelson, George Clooney,** *O Brother, Where Art Thou?*, 2000

⚜ 1930s Hollywood starlet

1930–1939

The most popular foundation in this period was ivory with a hint of pink. In the early part of the decade, the rouge used was in pale pink shades; later on, the trend was for a darker rouge, in shades as deep as raspberry pink. Movie stars set the trends in what has often been called the golden age of Hollywood.

⊕ **Bette Davis,** portrait, c.1932, see page 190

⊕ **Jean Harlow,** portrait, 1934

⊕ **Marlene Dietrich,** portrait, 1936

⊕ **Greta Garbo,** portrait, 1932

⚜ 1930s leading man

1930–1939

Hollywood's leading men of the 1930s were well-groomed with minimal facial hair – at the most, a thin and neat moustache – and a healthy, glowing complexion. After the extravagance of the flappers and the Wall Street Crash of 1929, a sobriety overcame society across America and Europe, and the make-up of the period reflected this change in values.

⊕ **Errol Flynn,** portrait, c.1939, see page 194

⊕ **Cary Grant,** portrait

⊕ **Clark Gable,** portrait, 1934

⊕ **Robert Mitchum,** portrait

⚫ WWII forces' sweetheart

1939–1945

Betty Grable's Technicolor movies of the 1940s made her the most popular pin-up girl of WWII. Glamorous actresses and singers, like Grable and Britain's Vera Lynn, opted for a natural look. They used slightly dark, warm-toned foundation with pinkish rouge, muted eyeshadow and fine eyeliner. Eyebrows were of a natural thickness but the arch was accentuated.

⊕ Gloria De Haven, 1944, see page 198

⊕ Patricia Roc, *Millions Like Us,* 1943

⊕ Betty Grable, portrait

⊕ Judy Garland, *For Me and My Gal,* 1942

⚫ 1940s glamour

1940–1949

When WWII came to an end, some cosmetics remained difficult to find and expensive to buy. As make-up became more easily affordable, the predominant look remained fairly natural. The exception was lipstick: one available colour plan was "contrast", a series of colours bringing a definite accent (often cherry or crimson) to the lip tone. A more natural look, often with reddish-orange tones, was provided by the "monotone" plan.

⊕ Scarlett Johansson, *The Black Dahlia,* 2006, see page 202

⊕ Veronica Lake, portrait, 1943

⊕ Lauren Bacall, portrait, 1943

⊕ Rita Hayworth, portrait, 1948

1950s housewife

1950–1959

The popular image of the 1950s housewife, heavily satirized in the book and movie *The Stepford Wives*, is currently enjoying a certain retro popularity. Floral dresses and a pile of blonde hair define the look. The make-up should appear fairly natural, but with bright lips setting off the brilliant smile.

⊕ **Ginger Rogers,** portrait

⊕ **Doris Day,** portrait, 1957, see page 206

⊕ **Lucille Ball, Desi Arnaz,** *I Love Lucy* (US TV series), 1951–1957

⊕ **Doris Day,** portrait, 1952

Blonde bombshell

1950–1959

Marilyn Monroe's dumb blonde persona made her the global superstar of her day, with the run of films beginning with *Gentlemen Prefer Blondes* exposing vast audiences to her trademark style. Marilyn's red pout and arched brows were unquestionably the look for would-be bombshells to copy in the mid-to-late 1950s.

⊕ **Mamie Van Doren,** portrait, 1956

⊕ **Jayne Mansfield,** portrait, see page 210

⊕ **Marilyn Monroe,** portrait

⊕ **Sheree North,** portrait

🌑 1950s glamour

1950–1959

The key innovation of this decade was the invention of the Max Factor "Pan Cake", a foundation to gloss over skin imperfections. Later in the decade, titanium was added to Max Factor products to tone down their brightness – resulting in lips with a pale shimmer. The idea was extended, and frosted nail varnishes in pink, silver and other colours were created.

⊕ **Ava Gardner,** portrait, 1952

⊕ **Elizabeth Taylor,** portrait, 1954, see page 214

⊕ **Audrey Hepburn,** portrait, 1953

⊕ **Grace Kelly,** portrait, 1954

🌑 Rock 'n' roll

1950–1969

The 1960s were a period of experimentation. Sideburns were in vogue and men's fashion of the rock 'n' roll period of the early sixties reflected a pre-adolescent, boyish charm. Later came the hippie movement and the Woodstock festival of 1969, its psychedelic apex. The origins of glam rock had been stirring since the 1950s, and in the late sixties Alice Cooper and his bandmates began to dress in gold lamé pants, and wear copious mascara.

⊕ **David Hemmings,** portrait, 1966

⊕ **Warren Beatty,** portrait, 1961, see page 222

⊕ **Michael Caine,** *The Italian Job*, 1969

⊕ **Dustin Hoffman,** portrait, 1967

☉ 1960s chick

1960–1969

Heavy eyes dominated the face. The eyebrows and lips were played down after the early 1960s when heavy, Egyptian brows were popular. The look of the period was characterized by false lashes (women wore two sets on top and one on the bottom), frosted pink lips (or any chalky colour), and heavy, slightly theatrical shading in the eye socket using a pale colour on the eyelid. No blusher was used, but the cheeks were shaded under the cheekbone.

⊕ **Faye Dunaway,** portrait, 1967

⊕ **Brittany Snow,** *Hairspray,* 2007, see page 218

⊕ **Julie Andrews,** portrait, 1966

⊕ **Veruschka,** *Blow Up,* 1966

☉ 1970s disco

1970–1979

A soft, natural look with long eyelashes was popular – though for disco nights, a more stylized and glittery appearance was created. Lipliner was often worn without lipstick, keeping the colour of the lips relatively natural but making them appear fuller, and with a more definite bow shape.

⊕ **Pam Dawber,** portrait, 1978

⊕ **Farrah Fawcett,** *Charlie's Angels* (US, TV series), 1976–1981, see page 226

⊕ **Tamara Dobson,** *Cleopatra Jones,* 1973

⊕ **Susan Dey,** *The Partridge Family* (US, TV series), 1970–1974

⚫ 1980s power dressing

1980–1989

The strong, even exaggerated, shapes and colours of women's dress were mirrored in their make-up. Bright lips and shocking pink eyeshadow were common. A favourite cosmetic of the decade was Clarins' Beauty Flash, a facial pick-me-up used to erase signs of fatigue.

⊕ **Melanie Griffith,** *Working Girl*, 1988

⊕ **Morgan Fairchild,** portrait, c.1980, see page 230

⊕ **Kim Cattrall,** *Mannequin*, 1987

⊕ **Katey Sagal,** *Married with Children* (US, TV series), 1987–1997

⚫ 1980s men's fashion

1980–1989

Men in the 1980s paid more attention to style and grooming than had been normal before in this century. Designer stubble made its first appearance, a trend started by Don Johnson's character in the TV show *Miami Vice*. It remained very rare for men outside Hollywood film sets and TV studios ever to wear make-up – but skincare and hairstyling products were popular.

⊕ **David Hasselhoff,** *Baywatch* (US, TV series), 1989–2001

⊕ **Patrick Swayze,** portrait, 1988, see page 234

⊕ **Matthew Broderick,** *Ferris Bueller's Day Off*, 1986

⊕ **Val Kilmer,** *Top Gun*, 1986

ⓘ 1980s girls' fashion

1980–1989

Madonna wannabes in the early 1980s took the self-styled Material Girl as their make-up icon, copying her pale-skinned, red-lipped, and bushy-browed style. Other celebrity figures inspired the exaggerated styles of the decade, which is most notable for the heavy eyeshadow often worn in bright shades of pink and green.

Michelle Pfeiffer, *Scarface*, 1983

⊕ **Madonna,** *Desperately Seeking Susan*, 1985, see page 238

⊕ **Daryl Hannah,** *Splash*, 1984

Cher, *Moonstruck*, 1987

ⓘ 1990s glamour

1990–2005

The look of this decade was overwhelmingly natural – foundations became lighter and lighter, making them steadily less obvious, and the lips were stained less vibrantly than in the 1980s. The runaway success story of the 1990s was Yves St. Laurent's Touche Éclat – a pen-brush used for shading and highlighting, banishing shadows and signs of fatigue.

Meg Ryan, *You've Got Mail*, 1998

⊕ **Jennifer Aniston,** portrait, c.2005, see page 242

⊕ **Sandra Bullock,** portrait, 1991

⊕ **Heather Locklear,** portrait, 1992

🌑 1990s grunge

1990–1995

Grunge was part of a broader trend sometimes called anti-fashion. Devotees of grunge eschewed heavy make-up and overly stylized appearances. This muted style is a deliberate reaction against the flashier aesthetic of the 1980s, which had prized fashion-consciousness in men and exaggerated make-up in women.

⊕ **Brad Pitt,** portrait, 1993

⊕ **Matthew Fox,** *Party of Five* (US, TV series), 1994–2000, see page 246

⊕ **Winona Ryder,** *Reality Bites*, 1994

⊕ **Adam Sandler, Brendan Fraser, Steve Buscemi,** *Airheads*, 1994

🌑 Bollywood

1990–2005

The Bollywood look is all about conspicuous glamour. Vivid eyeshadow, often in metallic shades; thick false lashes; generous, rose-coloured lips; and apricot-tinged cheeks will help to make a strong impression. A bindi secured with eyelash glue is an essential feature.

⊕ **Indira Varma, Naveen Andrews,** *Kama Sutra: A Tale of Love*, 1996

⊕ **Vasundhara Das,** *Monsoon Wedding*, 2001, see page 250

⊕ **Aishwarya Rai,** *Bride and Prejudice*, 2004

⊕ **Tabu,** *The Namesake*, 2006

Prehistoric

YOU WILL NEED

- Tail comb
- Crepe hair
- Spirit gum
- Scissors
- Pen or pencil
- Stage dirt
- Sponge
- Red greasepaint

1 Prepare crepe hair for the moustache (see page 24), and glue on with spirit gum, pressing against the upper lip with the arm of a tail comb or pen. ➲

2 Trim the moustache to the desired length. ➲

3 Lengthen the width of the moustache by applying spirit gum to the sides of the lip, and laying hair. To fix, apply pressure with a sideways rolling motion, using the end of a pen. ➲

4 To lay the beard, apply spirit gum just below the bottom lip and lay hair, pressing on firmly. ⬇

5 Work backwards, laying hair from the corner of the mouth up along the jawline until you reach the sideburns. ⬆

6 Rather than trimming, paint a line of spirit gum under the jawline and fold the ends of the beard back under the chin and jaw, pressing them into the glue. ⬆

7 Apply red greasepaint using a stipple sponge. ➡

8 With your finger, press stage dirt onto the high points of the face, including the cheekbones and brow. ⬇

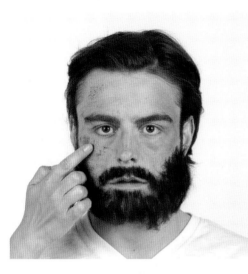

9 Blend the stage dirt in roughly but not too much – it needs to remain visible as dirt. ⬆

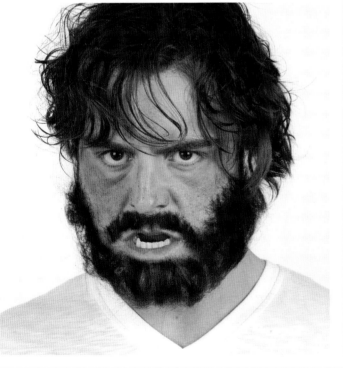

PRO TIP

Gluing the ends of a long beard back under the chin rather than trimming to the desired length gives the appearance of a fuller beard and suggests a longer period of hair growth, as well as adding to an ungroomed appearance. This method of laying hair can also be used if you are under time pressure or doing make-up for an extra.

Ancient Egypt

YOU WILL NEED

- → Warm foundation
- → Loose powder
- → Black eyeshadow
- → Black liquid liner
- → Grey eyeshadow
- → Peach blusher
- → Nude lipstick
- → Silver glitter
- → Ruler

1 Working on eyes first, blend some foundation as an eye base over the whole of the eye area; set with loose powder. The look has strong eyebrows so define and build up using a black pressed eyeshadow and a small angled brush. Keep the strokes short and work outwards from the nose, creating a shallow peak with a definite angle, using a ruler to get the top line as straight as possible. ↑

2 Using the ruler, draw a light line continuing from the end of the eyebrow at the same angle down towards the ear. ↑

3 Line all the way around the eye with black liquid liner, finishing at a point on the outer corner, and line the inner side of the bottom lid with a soft kohl pencil. ↓

4 Use the ruler to draw a straight line with the liquid liner from the outer corner of the bottom lash line at an angle of approximately 30 degrees until it meets the powder line drawn in step 2. ➡

6 Fill in the powder line between the two eyeliner lines and block out the space between the lines close to the outer corner of the eye. Blend dark grey eyeshadow over the whole lid up to the eyebrow and out as far as the powder line. Curl the eyelashes and apply two coats of mascara. ⬅

5 From the outer corner of the upper lash line, wing the eyeliner out with a slightly curved stroke to meet the powder line as in the previous step, about a pencil-width from the first line. ⬆

9 Finish off by filling in the empty space between the two eyeliner lines with silver glitter. ⊙

7 Clean up any fallen eyeshadow powder and then blend foundation over the rest of the face and set with loose powder; conceal where necessary. Enhance contours of the cheeks with a natural peach blusher, applied under the cheekbones. ⊕

8 Outline the lips with a natural lip pencil to define the shape and then apply a nude colour lipstick over whole lip and blot. ⊕

PRO TIP

With a heavy eye look do the eyes first so that you can clean the skin afterwards, should any shadow fall.

Ancient Greece

1 Apply a base (see page 17) using a lightweight foundation or tinted moisturiser. The base should not be too heavy, to reflect the period. Choose a warm tone. Conceal where necessary and use powder sparingly to set.

2 Groom the eyebrows to fill in and define, using a matt eyeshadow. ➔

3 Prepare the eye area with a nude cream eye base or eyeshadow, covering the whole area from the lashes to the brow. ➔

4 Use a soft black kohl pencil to line completely along the top eyelashes and on the lower eyelid. Go as far as the inner corner. Smudge the pencil line on top to soften the effect, using a clean eye detail brush. ➋

6 Apply mascara (see page 23). ⬇

5 Under the bottom lashes, apply a matt dark green eyeshadow powder. Extend the outer corner of the eyeline on the top eyelid outwards using this powder. Shade the eye socket with a reddish-brown matt powder and blend well. ⬆

7 Give the apples of the cheeks a flush of colour with reddish-brown blusher. ◔

8 Smudge a reddish-brown lipstick into the lips with your finger. ◔

PRO TIP

Clean under the eye using a cotton bud and use the powder you pick up on the cotton bud to extend the line of powder outwards from the corner of the eye.

Ancient Rome

1 Prepare the skin. Apply a base (see page 17) and conceal as necessary. Use a pale shade of medium-weight foundation – select one with a beige tint so as not to appear too theatrical. ⬇

2 Lightly powder the T-zone, to reduce shine, but do not powder the cheeks.

3 Prepare the eye area with a nude cream or powder eyeshadow. Highlight (see page 17) with a white shadow under the arch of the eyebrows. ⬆

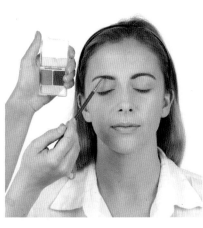

4 Groom the brows and, using a slanted brush, darken with a matt brown eyebrow powder or eyeshadow. Use small upward strokes, starting on the inner edge of the brows and working up to the high point of the arch. Make longer sweeps as you go over the arch and towards the outer points. The brows should look heavy. ⬅

5 Apply a matt taupe eyeshadow in the eye sockets. ⬆

6 Define the eyeline by adding a thin line of brown kohl pencil or gel eyeliner along the lashes. Curl the eyelashes and apply mascara (see page 23). ⬆

7 For a natural look, apply a cream blusher in a magenta shade, using a circular motion with the blusher brush to avoid the blusher taking on an angular appearance. Work the blusher over the apples of the cheeks and under the cheekbones, lifting it towards the top of the ear. ⬅

8 Stain the lips with a red lip colour. Lightly powder the whole face, blending the powder over the blusher, using loose powder and a large powder brush. ➲

PRO TIP

Brush Vaseline over the lips to give a more natural finish and blot to take away the shine.

Mayan girl

YOU WILL NEED

- Eyebrow pencil
- Black greasepaint, aquapaint or liquid eyeliner
- Beads or stones
- Surgical eyelash adhesive

1 Prepare the skin to ensure it is clean and oil-free. Finish with moisturiser. Apply a thin wash of warm base or tinted moisturiser to enhance the skin tone. ➔

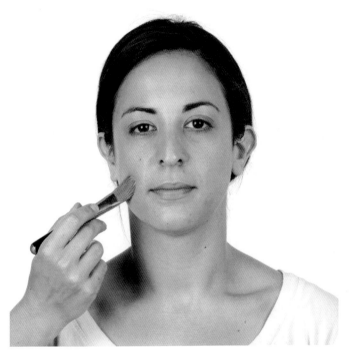

2 Conceal where necessary. ⬅

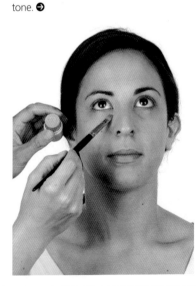

3 Lightly dust with loose translucent powder to set and remove shine, using a powder brush. ➔

4 Mark the shape of the face markings onto the skin using a light eyebrow pencil. ⬇

5 When you are happy with the shape of the markings, draw over the eyebrow pencil with black greasepaint, aquapaint or liquid eyeliner. ⬆

7 Press down firmly for thirty seconds. ➡

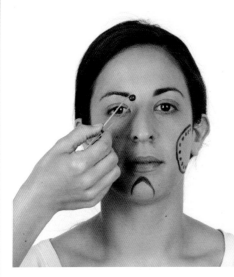

6 Stick beads or stones onto the face using surgical eyelash adhesive. Position with tweezers. ⬆

PRO TIP

Use a fine brush to draw on the markings roughly so they look like they have been drawn by hand. Aquapaint lasts longer than greasepaint but if you have neither, use liquid eyeliner.

Eastern warrior

YOU WILL NEED

- ➲ Bald cap
- ➲ Powder
- ➲ Crepe hair
- ➲ Spirit gum
- ➲ Pen
- ➲ Curling tongs

1 Create a bald head using a bald cap (see page 162). Powder to set. ⬇

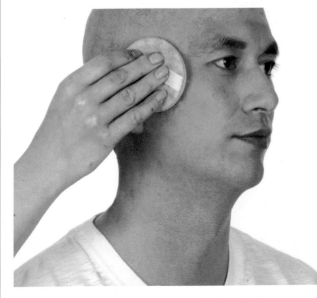

2 Begin laying the moustache by starting at the sides, laying hair quite long on top. Use spirit gum to lay the hair and trim down the sides. Hold a bunch of hair in your hand, apply the glue to the skin at the sides of the mouth and roll the hair off your finger. Press the hair on with a pen and roll it over the moustache using an inward roll. ⬆

3 Repeat the process, working inwards towards the middle of the top lip. Make sure each bunch of hair is a similar size so the density of the moustache is uniform. ⊖

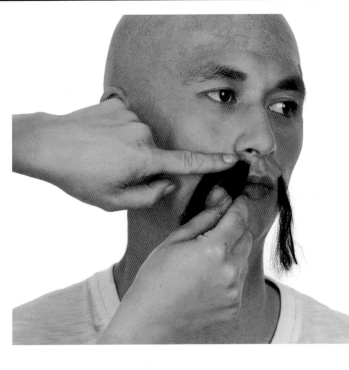

4 Leaving the outer pieces long, trim the hair along the top lip so it sits just above the lip. ⊙

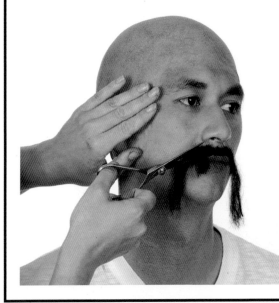

5 Lift the ends one at a time and curl them gently to get a natural shape. ⊙

6 Lay hair on the outer half of the eyebrow. ⬇

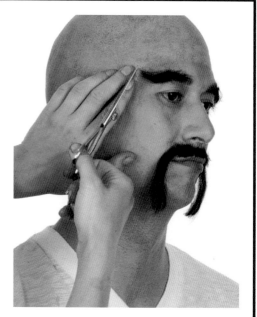

7 Trim eyebrows to the desired length and mould with your fingers. ⬆

PRO TIP

Work a little moustache wax into the crepe hair with your fingers to mould it to your desired shape and spray to set.

Celtic warrior

YOU WILL NEED

- ➔ Eyebrow pencil
- ➔ Blue aquapaint
- ➔ Cotton buds

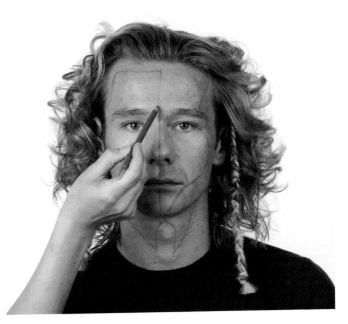

1 Begin by marking out your desired pattern using an eyebrow pencil. ⬆

2 Once you are happy with your design, go over the eyebrow pencil line with blue aquapaint, using a small synthetic brush. ⬅

3 Thicken the line with a bigger synthetic brush so that you don't go over the line when filling in with a big brush. Fill in the colour using blue aquapaint and a foundation brush, leaving some skin visible around the eye. ➔ + ⬇

4 Using a cotton bud, remove any aquapaint where you want the skin to show through, for example to resemble a scar. ⬆

PRO TIP

Work quickly when using aquapaint
to avoid it drying before you've
worked it around.

Italian Renaissance

YOU WILL NEED

- Brow powder
- Brown eyeshadow
- Kohl eyeliner
- Mascara
- Reddish-pink rouge
- Burned-pink lip stain

1 Prepare the skin, applying a base as described on page 17. Use a light foundation in a pale shade.

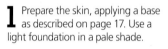

2 Apply concealer with a concealer brush where required (see page 16). Blend into the foundation with your finger. ➊ + ➋

3 Shade and highlight the face (see page 17) to improve the bone structure. ➌

4 Groom the eyebrows by combing through. Fill in the brows with brow powder in a shade compatible with the natural colour of the hairs. Use a slanted eyebrow brush and start on the inner corner. With small strokes of the brush, work outwards over the arch to the outer edge. ➜

5 Give the eyes depth by shading the socket line with a matt brown eyeshadow. Apply a little shadow at a time and blend well so no hard lines are visible. ⬆

6 Enhance the eyes by applying a dark brown or black kohl eyeliner close to the lashes on the top lids only. Curl the eyelashes and apply mascara. ➜

7 Italian women in the Renaissance often wore rouge circled heavily around the apples of their cheeks, but this look is slightly more subtle. Choose a reddish-pink tone and apply lightly, swirling over the apples. ⬇

8 Apply a burnt-red lip stain by dabbing lipstick onto the lips with your finger and blotting. This will give a natural finish. ↩

PRO TIP

Blusher can be powdered or cream, or if you have neither in the desired tone, use a dab of lipstick of the appropriate shade and work it into the skin using your fingers.

Tudor England

YOU WILL NEED

- ➲ Eyebrow pencil
- ➲ Spirit gum
- ➲ Crepe hair
- ➲ Tail comb

1 Apply a light cream base to the face and neck (see page 18). Shade and highlight where necessary. ➲

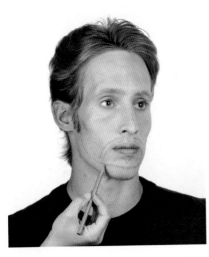

2 Mark on the shape of the facial hair using an eyebrow pencil. ➳

3 Paint spirit gum onto the skin in the area where you are going to attach the first bunch of hair. Wait for it to go tacky. ➲

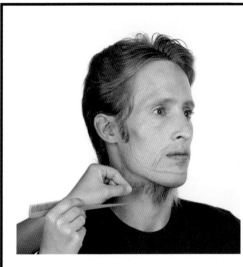

4 Attach sections of crepe hair, working outwards along the jawline. Use a tail comb to help stick small sections on. ⬅

5 Repeat steps 3 and 4 for the moustache. ➡

6 Work up along the jawline until the beard reaches the sideburns. ⬇

7 The final hair to be laid is the small tuft in the middle of the chin. ⬇

8 Trim the beard and moustache to the desired length to tidy the ends. ↪

PRO TIP

The correct way to lay a full beard is to lay the chin hair first, working from the neck forwards. Then lay the moustache hair over the top lip, followed by the hairs from the chin to the sideburns.

Elizabethan England

YOU WILL NEED

- White greasepaint
- Translucent powder
- White eyeshadow
- Red/brown eye pencil
- Subtle warm beige eyeshadow
- Soft brown powder
- Brick red lipstick
- Peachy blusher

1 Prepare the skin by applying a base over the face and neck, not forgetting the ears and eyelids. Use a pale shade, mixing white greasepaint into the whitest foundation. Apply the foundation using a foundation brush, and blend with your fingers. ⬆

2 Powder well using a translucent powder. ⬆

3 Contour to achieve an oval-shaped face – shade the jaw, and lightly shade the eye socket. Use something slightly darker than the white to shade the sides of the nose to make it as straight as possible, and the sides of the face for the perfect oval.

4 Highlight down the centre of the nose with a matt white eyeshadow. Brush some white through the eyebrows and onto the high point of the eyelids. Draw on high, thin brows using a red/brown eye pencil (the Queen used brown as she got older). ⬅

5 Line around the eyes with a soft brown powder. Emphasize the outer eye in order to draw the eyes apart. Do this using a small eye detail brush. ⬆

6 To clean away any fallen powder, brush through lashes with a clear mascara. (No emphasis on lashes.)

7 Brush a matt, peachy toned blusher over the cheekbones in an oval shape. ⬆

8 Lightly stain lips with a brick-red colour, keeping the shape rounded and small. Use a brush to apply, smudging in with the finger afterwards. Keep the colour concentrated at the centre, rather than going right to the corners of the mouth. ↩

PRO TIP

The eyebrows should look thin and wispy, but with a high arch. You may need to play down your model's eyebrows, depending on how dark they are. Try applying a thin layer of foundation over them.

Restoration

YOU WILL NEED

- Pale eyebrow pencil
- Crepe hair
- Spirit gum
- Tail comb
- Hair scissors
- Cotton wool
- Pencil
- Moustache wax

1 Do a straight make-up (see page 18). Mark the shape of the beard and moustache using a pale eyebrow pencil. Prepare crepe hair (see page 24) and lay on the chin, following the shape of the beard you wish to recreate. ➊

2 Use the tail end of a tail comb to guide you as you trim the beard to the correct length and into the desired shape, using hair scissors. ➊

3 Shape the beard with your fingers, and apply some moustache wax to hold the desired shape. ➋

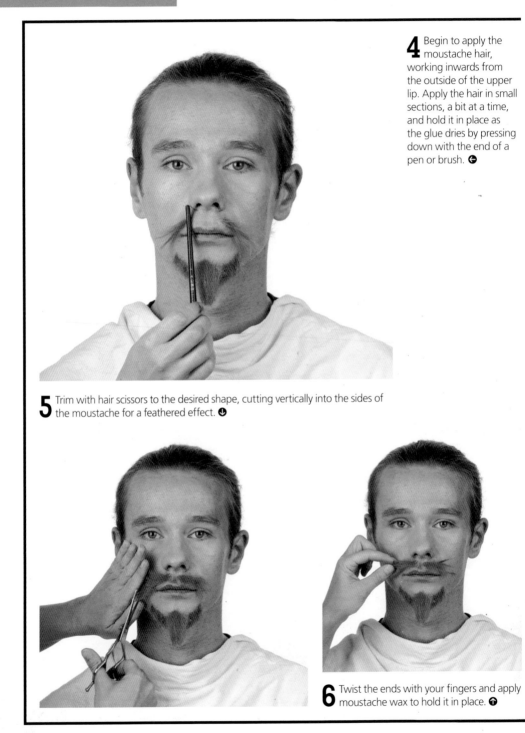

4 Begin to apply the moustache hair, working inwards from the outside of the upper lip. Apply the hair in small sections, a bit at a time, and hold it in place as the glue dries by pressing down with the end of a pen or brush. ↺

5 Trim with hair scissors to the desired shape, cutting vertically into the sides of the moustache for a feathered effect. ↻

6 Twist the ends with your fingers and apply moustache wax to hold it in place. ↑

PRO TIP

Men tend to grey around the temples first – by adding colour on the sideburns and temples you will be able to suggest age without altering the model's appearance drastically.

Gothic

YOU WILL NEED

- Black eyeshadow
- Nude beige eyeshadow
- Kohl eyeliner pencil or pot
- White greasepaint
- Ruby red lipliner
- Ruby red lipstick

1 Smudge black eyeliner along the top lash line using either a pencil or kohl liner in a pot and a flat liner brush. ⬆

3 Use a fine detail brush to line the lower eyelid close to the lash line. ➥

2 Brush a matt black eyeshadow over the eyeliner and smudge up towards the socket, blending the edges so the colour fades away. ⬆

4 Smudge the eyeshadow under the eyes with a clean brush. ⬆

5 Ask your model to look away and line around the eyes. ⬆

6 Blend in a nude matt beige eyeshadow just below the black eyeline. ⬆

7 Apply eyeliner to the inside of the lower eyelid using a black kohl pencil. ⬆

8 Clean the skin to remove any fallen eyeshadow. Use a foundation sponge to apply a pale foundation mixed with a small amount of white greasepaint. ⬆

9 Block out the corners of the lips using a very pale foundation or concealer. Powder, then draw the outline of a full, bow-shaped lip (see page 21). ⬇

10 Fill the lips in with lipstick, using a lip brush, and blot and repeat. ⬆

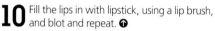

PRO TIP

Use any striking, dark lip colour – the gothic look was about originality more than anything else.

18th-century France (man)

YOU WILL NEED

- Pale cake make-up
- Damp sponge
- Loose translucent powder
- Velour puff
- Toothbrush
- Brow gel
- Hairspray
- Rust tone blusher
- Eyebrow pencil
- Brown-red matt lipstick

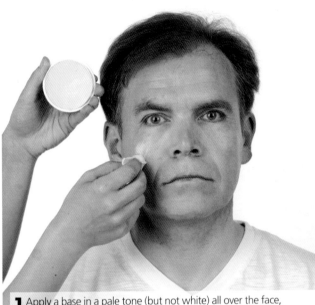

1 Apply a base in a pale tone (but not white) all over the face, including the eyelids. Use either a cream cake applied with a foundation brush and blended with fingers or an aquacolour applied with a damp sponge and worked quickly into the skin. ↑

2 Continue the application of base down over the neck and ears. ↑

3 Set with loose transculent powder. Press the powder into the skin using a velour puff and work it in until the powder disappears. ➔

4 Groom the eyebrows with a toothbrush and brush the hairs on the inner half upwards and those towards the outside downwards to exaggerate the arch. Set with brow gel or by spraying a little hairspray onto your fingers and smoothing over. ⬇

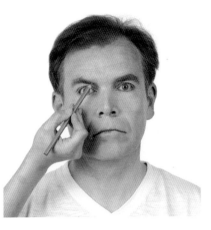

6 To strengthen the brow further you can lightly pencil through with an eyebrow pencil. ⬆

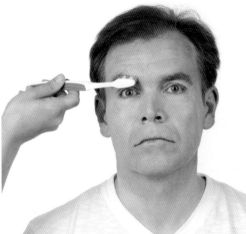

5 Apply a small amount of blusher in a rust tone, circling it over the apples of the cheeks, and blending it downwards down the sides of the nose. Use a blusher brush with powder blusher or fingers if using cream blusher or greasepaint. ⬇

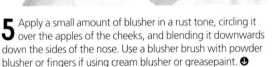

7 Smudge a small amount of matt lipstick in a brown-red shade onto the lips with a lip brush. Work well into the lips and blot. It should just look like a wash of colour. ⬆

PRO TIP

Don't forget to match the neck and
ears to the face in colour, using the
same base foundation and translucent
powder. Shade and highlight for a
longer face.

18th-century France

YOU WILL NEED

- ➔ Pale foundation
- ➔ Matt taupe eyeshadow
- ➔ Matt brown eyeshadow
- ➔ Brown mascara
- ➔ Eyebrow powder
- ➔ Pinky matt blusher
- ➔ Natural pink lipstick
- ➔ Dusky rose lipstick

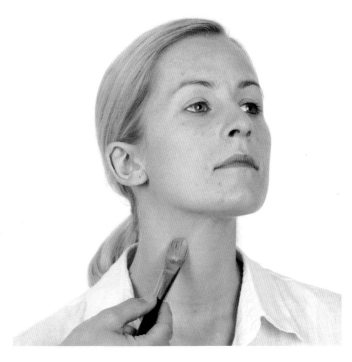

1 Apply the foundation with a foundation brush, starting in the centre and blending out towards the edges. Apply the base over the eyelids and set lightly by dusting the whole face with translucent powder. ➔

2 Prepare the eye area by brushing a nude eyeshadow all over the eye from the lash line to the brow. Apply a matt taupe eyeshadow all over the eye and shade the socket. ➔

3 Using a matt brown powder and a detail brush, softly line around the eye. ➔

4 There is no need to curl the eyelashes – one coat of brown mascara on the top lashes will suffice.

5 Fill the eyebrows using brow powder. Use short strokes with an angled brush, starting from the inside and working to the outside to make them look thicker. ⊖

6 Apply a pinky matt blusher over the cheekbone in an oval shape. ⊖

7 Create softly bowed lips in a natural pink shade by outlining (see page 20) and filling with a pencil. Use lipstick over the top in a dusky rose colour, and blot. ↩

PRO TIP

This look is tailored to suit modern-day audiences – if the look was too pale, audiences would not enjoy looking at it. The look recreated here is toned down for audience comfort so is not typical of the period.

Regency England

YOU WILL NEED

- ➔ Pale base
- ➔ Translucent powder
- ➔ Eyebrow wand
- ➔ Taupe eyeshadow
- ➔ Red-based blusher
- ➔ Brown eyeshadow
- ➔ Nude lip pencil
- ➔ Red lip pencil
- ➔ Red lipstick
- ➔ Liquid eyeliner

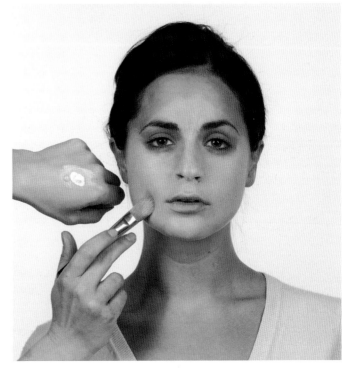

1 Apply a pale liquid base (see page 17) using a foundation brush – you could try mixing white into your palest foundation to achieve the correct colour. ➔

2 Set with translucent white powder using a velour puff. Press the puff against the face and roll the powder into the skin, repeating until it disappears. ➔

3 Groom the eyebrows with a wand and define their arched shape with an eyebrow pencil, but do not add any width – Georgian women preferred very thin eyebrows. ➔

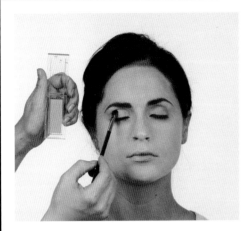

4 Prepare the eye area by applying foundation over the eyelid and setting with translucent powder. Give the eye shape and depth by shading the socket with a taupe eyeshadow. ⬆

5 Define the eye by lining around the lashline on the top and bottom lids with a matt brown eyeshadow, lifting the brow to get to the root of the lashes. ⬆

6 Apply one coat of mascara, taking care not to layer it too thickly.

7 Apply a red-based blusher sparingly with a blusher brush – circle it on just below the apples of the cheeks. Georgian women wore rouge in a rounded shape quite low down the cheek. ⬇

8 Draw on a lipline with a nude lip pencil to obtain the correct shape. Start with the bow, drawing inwards one side at a time, making it neat and rounded. Draw in the outer edges from the outside inwards so the line is solid. Draw the lips narrower than the model's, so they appear fuller. Repeat on the bottom lip. ⬇

9 When the lipline is correct, go over it with a red pencil and fill in with lipstick. Blot for a matt finish. ⬆

10 Replicate a Georgian face patch – used to cover blemishes or marks – using liquid eyeliner. Here it is worn close to the eye and looks much like a beauty spot. ⬆

PRO TIP

Place the hand you are not using under the model's chin so you can rest your drawing hand against it to keep it steady.

YOU WILL NEED

- Light matt grey eyeshadow
- Liquid eyeliner
- Eyelash curlers
- Mascara
- Surgical adhesive
- Brow powder
- Matt contouring blusher
- Rosy pink blusher
- Lip pencil
- Satin lipstick
- False eyelashes

Imperial Russia

1 Prepare the skin to ensure it is clean and oil-free, and finish with a foundation primer or oil-free moisturiser (see page 16).

2 Prepare the eye area by applying a thin layer of foundation and setting with powder. Use an eyeshadow brush to apply a light matt grey eyeshadow from the lashes to the socket. Blend the shadow upwards slightly above the socket towards the outer corner. ⬆

3 Line along the top lashes using a liquid eyeliner. The line should be neat, thin and close to the lashes. ⬆

4 Curl the lashes and apply one coat of mascara to the top only. ⬆

5 Using surgical adhesive, apply a set of half lashes to the outside part of the eyes (see page 22). ⬆

6 When the lash glue is dry, apply another coat of mascara and reline with the liquid liner. Open and brighten the eye by lining the inside of the lower lid with a white pencil. ⬆

7 Using a brow powder and slanted brush, define the eyebrows. Make short strokes with the eyebrush and work the powder into the natural hairs, starting on the outside and working inwards. ⬆

 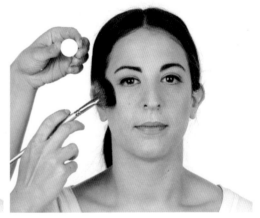

8 Contour under the cheeks, nose and chin to perfect the face shape (see page 17) using a matt contouring blusher in a skin tone. ⬆

9 Highlight the cheekbones (see page 17 for other areas to highlight) with a matt white eyeshadow, or a pale pressed powder. ⬆

10 Apply a rosy pink blusher over the apples of the cheeks, and blend back towards the ears. ⬇

11 Trace the outline of the lips with a lip pencil. The lips should be full and perfectly shaped (see page 21). Fill in with the pencil and then apply a nude satin lipstick. Blot and reapply. ⬅

PRO TIP

The skin should have a porcelain look. Choose a base that is pale and has a medium coverage.

Pirate

YOU WILL NEED

- Crepe hair
- Spirit gum
- Damp sponge
- Scissors
- Eyebrow pencil
- Kohl eyeliner pencil
- Beads

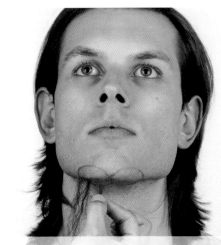

1 Prepare the skin to ensure it is clean and oil-free. If necessary, ask the actor or model to shave (it is harder to remove the spirit gum if the actor has stubble). Apply a very thin wash of base all over with a damp sponge (see page 18). Set with powder, and lightly dust. Prepare the crepe hair (see page 24), making sure the sections of hair are at least 8 cm long. With a light eyebrow pencil, mark the shape of the chin beard on the face. Glue under the chin with spirit gum and begin laying the hair a small bunch at a time, working backwards in rows, from the point of the chin towards the neck. ➊

2 Press the hair into the glue by rolling over the hair with a pen or the handle of a brush. When all the hair has been laid, wait a few minutes and press a clean towel over the whole area. Gently pull out any loose hairs. ➊

3 Twist the glued hair into two tendrils, using moustache wax to hold the hairs in place. Trim the ends. ➋

4 Mark the shape of the moustache with an eyebrow pencil. ⬇

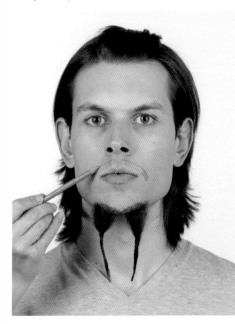

5 Paint on a thin layer of spirit gum and allow to dry. Paint on a second layer of glue on the side you're going to lay first. Lay the prepared hair (see page 25), working from the outside towards the centre, a small bunch at a time. ⬆

6 Continue working from the outside in, towards the middle. ⬆

7 When all the hair has been laid, trim to the desired length and cut into the moustache vertically to thin the edges, for a more natural look. ⬆

8 Ring around the eyes along the top and under the bottom lashes with a black soft kohl pencil, then smudge with your finger for a dishevelled look. ⬇

9 Thread beads onto the ends of the tendrils. ⬆

PRO TIP

Coat scissors and fingers with Vaseline to prevent them sticking together and becoming covered in glue.

Wild-west girl

YOU WILL NEED

- Tinted moisturiser
- Soft, brown eyeliner pencil or kohl pot
- Bronzer
- Nude beige eyeshadow powder or cream
- Mascara
- Rose-pink blusher
- Lipliner
- Vaseline

1 Apply a base all over the face (see page 17) using a tinted moisturiser in a warm shade. Conceal where necessary. ➊

2 Lightly set with loose powder on the T-zone.

3 Apply a golden shade of bronzer on the high points of the face, where the sun naturally colours the skin – across the top of the nose, on the apples of the cheeks and on the forehead and chin. ➊

4 Add freckles to the cheeks and the bridge of the nose, using a soft brown eyeliner pencil or kohl from a pot applied using a fine detail brush. ➡

5 Prepare the eye area with a nude beige powder or cream eyeshadow. Apply from the lash line to the brow, to neutralize the colour of the eye and absorb any excess oil. ⬇

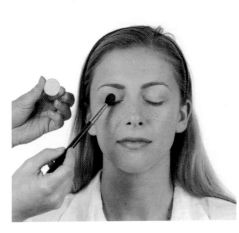

6 Groom the eyebrows. There is no need to darken them or add volume for this look. Apply brown eyeliner along the upper lash line using a kohl pencil. Work from the outer edge inward, and then back out toward the outer edge. Work over the line with a detail brush to ensure you have a solid, unbroken line. ⬆

7 Curl the eyelashes and apply one coat of mascara. ⬇

8 Apply a rose-pink blusher to the apples of the cheeks. Lightly touch the blusher brush into the product and dab onto the apples, building up the application a little at a time. ➡

9 To enhance and define the natural lip line, work around the edge of the mouth, outside of the lip line, using a concealer slightly lighter than the skin, and blend outwards. ⬇

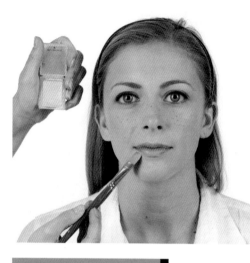

10 Draw on the lip line using a light pink lip pencil, then fill in the whole lip area with the same pencil. Add Vaseline on top. To finish, lightly powder the whole face with a loose, translucent powder. ⬆

PRO TIP

Ask the model to smile so you have a guide as to where to apply the blusher.

Wild-west man

YOU WILL NEED

- → Cream foundation
- → Tail comb
- → Spirit gum
- → Hair scissors
- → Crepe hair
- → Stubble wax

1 Prepare the skin to ensure it is clean and oil-free. Apply a subtle base (see page 18). Aquapaint is a good base for men – this is applied with a wet sponge and worked in quickly before the water evaporates. ⬇

3 Use the tail of a tail comb to lift the actor's own sideburn hair, and clip it out of the way with a sectioning clip. ⬇

2 Apply powder to set the base. ⬆

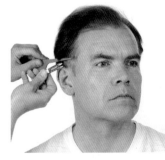

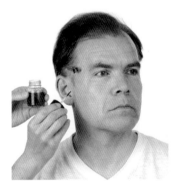

4 Paint spirit gum onto the skin where you are going to lay extra hair. ⬆

5 To extend the sideburns, lay prepared crepe hair (see page 25). Lay the hair one side at a time, starting at the bottom. Add a second layer of spirit gum to a small area, and apply more crepe hair. ⬇

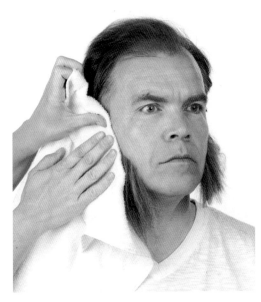

6 When all the hair has been laid, wait a few minutes and press down with a clean, dry towel. ⬆

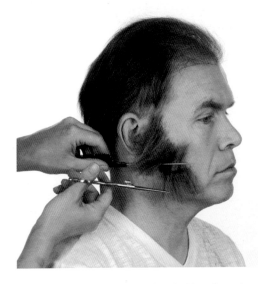

7 Use the tail of a thin tail comb to hold sections of hair out of the way, and trim the crepe hair to the desired length. ⬆

8 Lay a small tuft of crepe hair on the centre of the chin. ⬆

9 Apply a thin layer of stubble wax to the chin and upper lip areas. ⊙

10 Chop up some crepe hair into small pieces. Pick up some hairs on a dome brush, and press into the stubble wax on the face. ⊛

PRO TIP

For a weathered look, mix in some lighter coloured hair to give a grey effect, apply some bronzer and highlight wrinkles.

YOU WILL NEED

- Spirit gum
- Crepe hair
- Hair scissors
- Moustache wax

Napoleonic

1 Cleanse skin and apply a base (see page 18). Prepare crepe hair (see page 24). Paint a base layer of spirit gum onto the skin over the area where the moustache will be applied (see page 25). ↑

2 Lay the crepe hair a small bunch at a time, working from the outside inwards. Grasp the hair between your thumb and forefinger, and roll it slightly to fan out the ends. Paint a second layer of glue onto the area where you are going to lay the hair, and push the ends into the glue. ↑

3 Use the end of a pen or brush to secure the freshly laid hair, rolling outwards from the centre. ➔

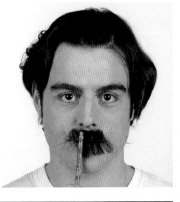

4 Before the glue dries completely, separate the hairs in the middle, and gently smooth into a shape that resembles curtains. ⬆

5 Trim the hair to the desired length. ⬆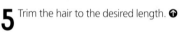

6 Groom the hair with your fingers, twisting the ends into a point. Hold the hair in this shape by applying moustache wax. ⬆

19th-century Pari

1 Prepare the skin and apply a base (see page 17). Apply an eye base using a nude cream eyeshadow. Work it into the eyelid from the lash line to the eyebrow. ➊

2 Lift the eyebrow to stretch the skin, and draw along the lash line using a black eyeliner pencil. First work upwards from the outer corner towards the nose, and then go over the line working from the inner corner outwards. ➊

3 Apply matt charcoal eyeshadow to the eyelid. When the model's eye is closed, the shape of the eyeshadow should resemble a petal. Apply the shadow onto the whole eyelid, slightly above the socket on the outer corner. Blend the edges to soften. ➌

4 Curl the eyelashes, and apply one coat of mascara. Attach false eyelashes to the outer half of the eyelid (see page 22). When the glue is completely dry, apply another coat of mascara to join the natural and false lashes. ↩

5 Conceal where necessary. ↑

6 Apply contouring blusher under the cheekbones to enhance their shape. Also apply it lightly down the sides of the nose and under the jawbone. ➋

7 Add colour by swirling a pink blusher over the apples of the cheeks and brushing downwards slightly on both sides of the nose. ⊙

8 Carefully draw on the lip line with a red pencil, perfecting the model's natural shape. Fill in with red lipstick. ⊖

PRO TIP

Blot the lipstick and apply a second coat for a longer lasting finish.

Victorian lady

YOU WILL NEED

- Light brown matt powder
- Matt white eyeshadow
- Matt taupe eyeshadow
- Mascara
- Matt pink blusher
- Pink lipstick

1 Prepare skin by applying a base of the palest foundation (not overly white) and conceal where necessary. Aim for a matt, even finish, contouring if necessary to improve structure. Powder to set. ⬆

2 Using an eyeshadow brush, apply a nude matt eyeshadow all over the eyelid from the lash line to the eyebrow, pressing the shadow into the skin. ⬆

3 Highlight the high point of the eyelid under the arch of the eyebrow using a matt white eyeshadow. Lightly shade the socket with a matt taupe eyeshadow. ⬅

4 Define along the upper and lower lash lines with a light brown matt powder (apply with a small eye detail brush). Apply one coat of mascara for grooming – it should not add too much definition. ⬆

5 Apply a matt pink blusher with a big brush in a circular motion to the centre of the cheeks. ⬆

6 For bee-stung, stained lips apply pink lipstick using a brush and blot. For a natural shape, use just lipstick and do not line the lips. ↩

PRO TIP

When defining along the bottom lash line, point the brush up towards the lid, lining beneath the lashes, close to the roots, using the lashes as a guide.

Poor Victorian

YOU WILL NEED

- Stage dirt or charcoal powder
- Purple greasepaint
- Tooth enamel
- Nicotine and black tooth colour

2 Dust the face lightly with translucent powder to set the make-up. Avoid creating an overly powdered appearance. ⬇

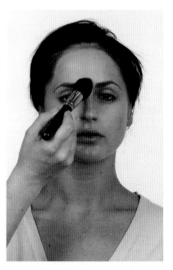

1 Apply the palest foundation in your kit (see page 17). The look is pale and undernourished, but not the pure white used for aristocratic or heavily theatrical looks. Therefore a very pale foundation is better than white stage make-up. Buff the foundation into the skin with a stipple foundation brush for a natural finish, blending it over the jawline, down the neck, and over the ears. ⬆

3 Break down the skin with stage dirt or charcoal powder. Apply the dirt to the face using a stipple sponge and work it in with the tips of your fingers by tapping them lightly over the face. ➜

4 Create dark circles around the eyes by applying purple greasepaint with a detail brush under the eyes where natural shadows would occur. Enhance the colour around the inner corners of the eyes and deepen any natural lines by painting greasepaint into them. ⬇

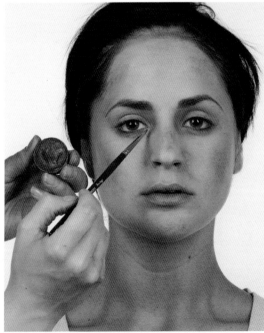

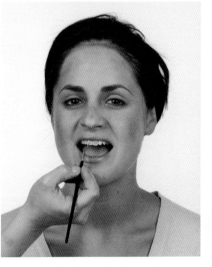

5 Break down the teeth with tooth enamel. Begin by drying the front teeth with tissue. Using a small brush, paint on a nicotine tooth colour. Allow to dry before dotting black tooth colour over the top. ⬆

PRO TIP

When applying stage dirt, don't apply it uniformly all over the face – you want a grubby and uneven look.

Victorian colonial

YOU WILL NEED

- ● Sectioning clips
- ● Spirit gum
- ● Crepe hair
- ● Fine tail comb
- ● Hair scissors
- ● Spatula
- ● Towel

1 Cleanse and prepare the skin. ↑

3 Clip the model's own sideburns out of the way using sectioning clips. ↓

2 Powder to set – use a velour puff and dust away any excess with a powder brush. ↑

4 Apply spirit gum to those areas of the face to which you will attach the crepe hair. ↑

5 Begin to lay the hair, working up along the jawline to the sideburns. ⊙

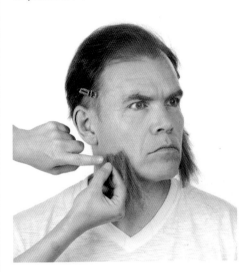

6 Roll over the hair as you lay it with a pen or the handle of a brush to secure the hairs. ⊙

7 Wait for a couple of minutes and press down firmly with a clean towel. ⊙

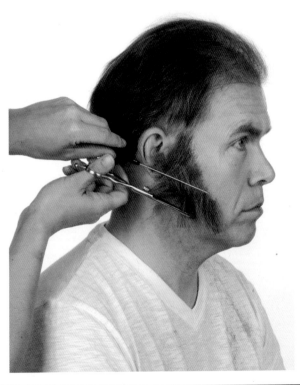

8 Use the end of the fine tail comb and some hairdressing scissors to trim the beard to the desired length. ➋

9 Start to lay the hair over the top lip, working from the outer corners upwards. Continue from the bottom of the side whiskers, laying a small bunch at a time. ⊙

10 Gently pull the hairs to remove any loose ones, then trim to the desired length. Cut into the moustache vertically to thin the edges. ⊙

PRO TIP

You might need to add some hair to the eyebrows to match the heaviness of the moustache. If you choose to do this, work outwards from the centre of each eyebrow.

US Civil War soldier

YOU WILL NEED

- Grey-blue greasepaint
- Stipple sponge
- Crepe hair
- Soft powder brush
- Pen
- Spirit gum
- Towel
- Tail comb
- Hair scissors
- Stage dirt
- Curling tongs

1 Apply straight make-up for men (see page 18). Darken the beard line with grey-blue greasepaint using a stipple sponge. ⊕

2 Stipple on moustache wax and finely chopped crepe hair around the jawline, using a soft powder brush. ⊕

3 Lay a moustache along the lip and up towards the nose, starting in the middle. Cut a piece of prepared crepe hair approximately 4 cm long, and trim the top so the edge is very blunt, with no loose hairs. Grasp the bunch of hair between your thumb and forefinger, rolling it slightly to fan out the ends. Push the ends of the hair into the spirit gum. ⊖

4 Once you have finished laying the hair, roll the end of a pen or brush over to fix it in place. Trim the bottom layer of hair so it does not irritate the model. ⬆ + ➡

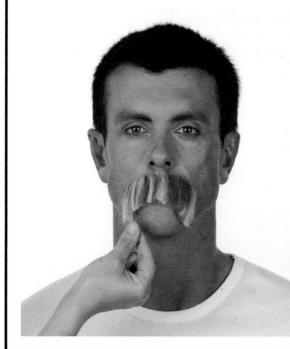

5 Roll the ends of loose hair around heated tongs before gluing them onto the skin so they will lift away from the lip slightly. Trim to the desired length and cut vertically into the moustache to thin the edges. ⬆

6 Build the hair up in layers along the lip first and then working upwards towards the nose. Use different shades of hair – darker on the base and becoming blonder on top. After gluing, pull out any loose hairs. ➡

7 Create under-eye bags using blue eyeshadow applied with a brush to the inner eye orbital bone and blend with a finger. ⬆

PRO TIP

The way a moustache is laid depends on the final desired shape and heaviness. Start laying it at the sides for a wispy moustache, or in the middle and in layers for a thicker moustache.

8 Stipple on stage dirt or "plains dust". ⬆

US Civil War lady

YOU WILL NEED

- Matt taupe eyeshadow
- Matt beige eyeshadow
- Matt white eyeshadow
- Brow powder
- Mascara
- Peach-toned blusher
- Nude lip pencil
- Satin-finish nude lipstick

1 Prepare the skin and apply a base (see page 17). Set with loose translucent powder. Roll into the skin using a velour puff.

2 Use a fan brush to dust a layer of loose powder onto the cheekbones. This will protect the base from any falling eyeshadow. ➔

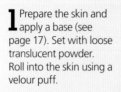

3 Apply a matt beige eyeshadow over the whole eye area from the lashes to the eyebrow. Highlight under the brow, in the inner corners of the eye and on the high point of the eyelid with a matt white eyeshadow. ⬆

4 With taupe eyeshadow, add depth to the eye by shading the socket from the outer edge to the inner corner. Blend the edges with a clean brush so there are no hard lines. ⬇

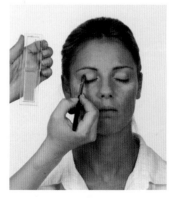

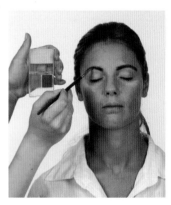

5 Groom the eyebrows. Take an appropriate shade of brow powder and, starting at the inner corner of the brow, use small swift strokes to fill and enhance the brow. Make it so that the outer part of the brow curves gently downwards. ⬆

6 Lightly apply one coat of mascara (see page 23), making sure that the lashes are clean and separated. ⬇

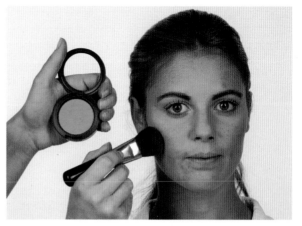

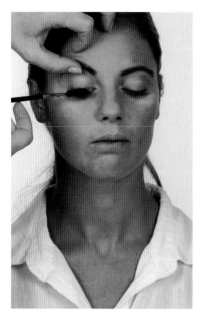

7 Brush away any loose powder from the cheekbones with a fan brush, and apply a healthy peach-toned blusher under the cheekbones, sweeping backwards towards the top of the ear with small circular movements. ⬆

8 Use a matt white powder to highlight the top of the cheekbone and centre of the nose. ⬇

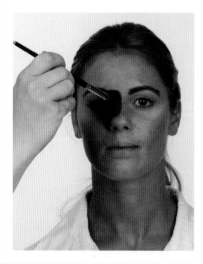

9 The bow of the lips needs to be very rounded in a sweetheart shape. To achieve this, first block out the model's own lipline with foundation. ⬆

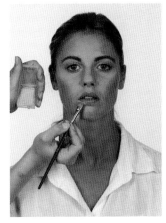

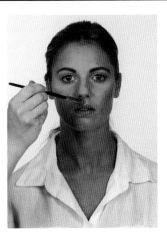

10 Draw in the new lip shape with a nude pencil. Start in the middle, drawing each side of the bow inwards (see page 20). ⬆

11 Fill in the lips with pencil. Add a satin-finish lipstick on top. ⬆

12 Use a light concealer to highlight around the outside of the lips and in the dip between the bow of the lips and the nose. ⬆

PRO TIP

When applying mascara, ask the model to look down. With your other hand, lift the brow slightly so that you can get to the root of the lashes.

YOU WILL NEED

- ➔ Cake base
- ➔ Crepe hair
- ➔ Spirit gum
- ➔ Scissors
- ➔ Black and purple greasepaint
- ➔ Stage dirt or loose brown eyeshadow
- ➔ Nicotine and black tooth enamel

Rasputin

1 Prepare the skin. Apply a thin wash of base all over using a cream cake base or water-based cake with a damp sponge. Work down the neck. Do not conceal. Set with loose powder, lightly dusting over with a powder brush. Select the appropriate colours of crepe hair and prepare the hair (see page 24). When ironing the hair to prepare it, press but do not straighten completely. ➔

2 Lay the hair for a long beard and moustache (see page 126). When you have finished laying the hair, gently pull to remove any loose hairs. Trim the beard and turn the scissors to vertical. Cut into the ends to soften the edges. ➔

3 Blacken around the eyes with greasepaint, using your fingers to smudge it into the socket and over the eyelid. With a flat liner or detail brush, apply the grease close to the lower lash line. Use purple greasepaint to emphasize the shadows on the inner corner and under the eye. ➔

4 Using stage dirt or a loose brown eyeshadow, dirty around the nose and the skin on the cheeks and forehead. Apply with a stipple sponge, and smudge into the skin with your fingers. ⬆

5 Add a dirty appearance to the teeth with tooth enamel. Begin by drying the front teeth with tissue. Using a small brush, paint on a nicotine tooth colour. ⬇

6 Allow to dry before dotting black tooth colour over the top using your finger. ⬅

PRO TIP

Laying just one colour of crepe hair will make the beard and moustache look unnatural, so mix two or more colours for a natural effect. When you have finished, if any hairs are not lying correctly they can be removed with tweezers.

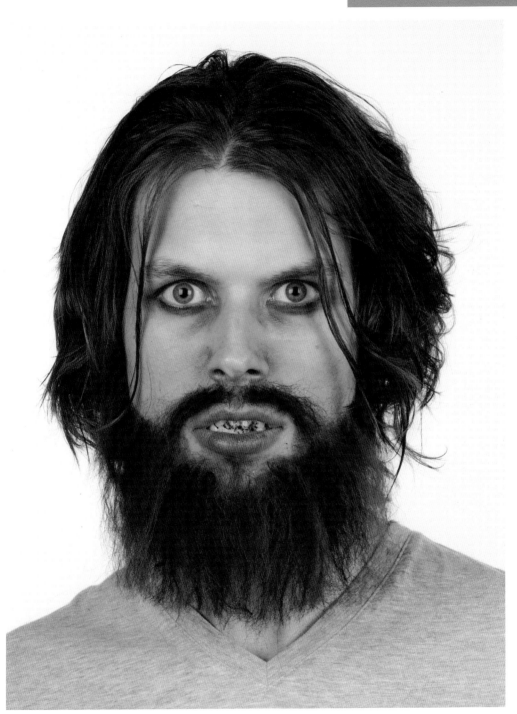

Native American

YOU WILL NEED

- Bald cap
- Scotch tape
- Eyebrow pencil
- Sharp scissors
- Hair gel
- Spirit gum
- Stipple sponge
- Rose pink aquapaint
- White aquapaint

1 Create a bald head using a bald cap. First, make sure the model's own hair is gelled and combed down. Clean the skin using a toner and make sure that it is dry. ⬆

3 Cut away the bulk of the extra cap at the front and tuck in any stray hairs. ⬇

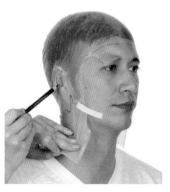

2 Ask the model to hold the front of the bald cap as you stretch it over from behind. It should sit just above the eyebrows. ⬆

4 Tape the sides of the cap down to hold it in place using Scotch tape. Draw a cutting line using eyebrow pencil, drawing inside the ear and around the sideburns. ⬆

5 Follow the cutting line to trim away the excess latex across the front of the cap. ⬇

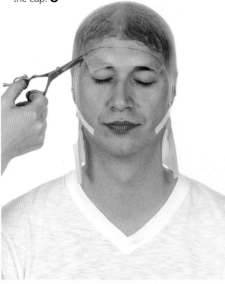

6 Glue under the edges of the cap with spirit gum, and push the cap down onto the forehead with a velour puff. Remove the tape and glue the side flaps. ⬆

7 Put some tape at the back of the neck, cut out inside the ear, following the line and tuck the cap behind the ear. ⬇

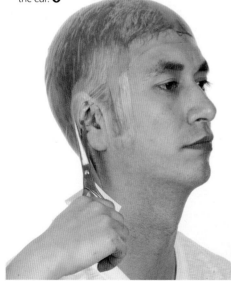

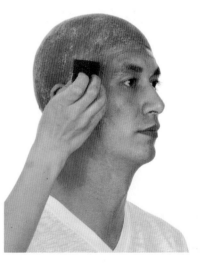

8 Use a stipple sponge to apply the aquacolour onto the cap. Use a rosy pink colour to counteract the colour of the hair beneath the cap. ⬆

9 When the aquacolour is dry, apply a foundation all over the face and cap and powder to set, pressing rather than dragging the foundation on the bald cap so as not to disturb the colour beneath. ⬇

10 Draw white lines onto the face to resemble war paint (use a finger if working with greasepaint and a brush if using a water-based paint). ⬅

PRO TIP

The paint should be applied non-symmetrically so it has a rough and ready look, as though it has been applied with a finger.

Geisha

YOU WILL NEED

- Mortician or nose wax
- Spirit gum
- White aquacolour
- Red greasepaint
- Dark eyebrow powder
- Liquid eyeliner
- Kohl pencil
- Mascara
- Red lipstick
- Tooth enamel (optional)

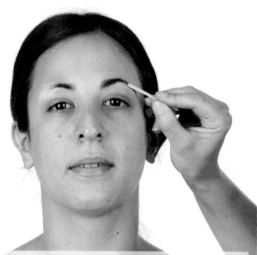

1 Block out the outer half of the eyebrows by grooming with a wand or eyebrow comb, and smoothing over the wax. If the hairs are thick and unruly, set them in place by combing and brushing over spirit gum. Paint a thin layer of mortician's wax over them. Warm the wax between your fingers, and smooth a thin layer over the hairs. Blend the edges into the skin with a spatula. ➊

2 Paint white aquacolour over the face, lips, neck and chest. Use a wet foundation brush, and work quickly so the water doesn't evaporate. ➊

3 Using a fine detail brush, mark a "W" on the back of the neck and fill in around it. ➌

5 Use dark eyebrow powder and a slanted brush to define the inner half of the eyebrow where the natural hairs are still visible. Extend the eyebrows in a straight line using liquid eyeliner or a kohl pencil. ⊙

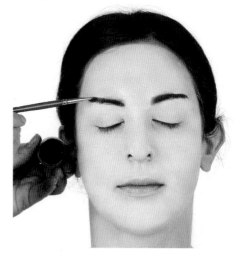

4 Extend the eyebrow line using red greasepaint or lipstick if nothing else is available. ⬆

6 The eyes are first lined in red. Use greasepaint and apply with a detail brush. Draw a "C" shape around the outer corner and fill in. ⬆

7 Line all the way around the eye, close to the lash line, with black liner. Groom the lashes and apply mascara (see page 23). ⬆

8 Paint the lips in a tight rosebud shape (see page 20) and blank out the outer edges of the lips with white paint. ⊙

9 Fill in with lipstick, blot and repeat. ⊙

PRO TIP

The juice from benibana or sallflower (beni) was used to redden the lips. To finish off this dramatic look, geisha would then blacken their teeth. This was achieved by staining the teeth with a mixture of oxidized iron filings steeped in an acidic solution. Application of this mixture would need to be repeated every couple of days or the teeth would return to white. To recreate this look, paint on a black tooth enamel.

Edwardian

YOU WILL NEED

- Taupe eyeshadow
- Dusky pink blusher
- Red lipliner and lipstick

1 Cleanse and prepare skin. Apply a pale but natural base (see page 17). Powder to set. ⬆

2 Use a taupe eyeshadow to shade the socket line, blending in the edges. ⬆

3 Use a liquid eyeliner to emphasize the eye shape by drawing a fine line along the top lashes. ⬅

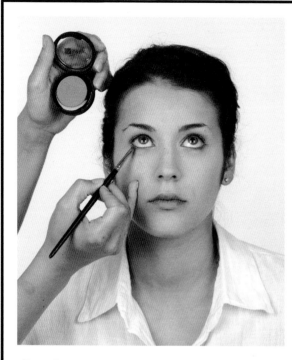

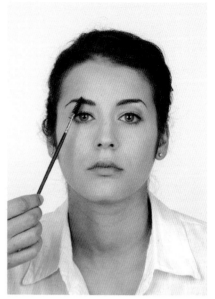

5 Groom the eyebrows using an eyebrow wand and pluck any stray hairs. ⬆

4 Use the taupe eyeshadow under the eyes to define and brighten them. Ask the model to look up, and smudge close to the lower lashes with a detail brush. ⬆

6 Apply a dusky pink blusher to the apples of the cheeks. ➔

7 Line and fill full red lips with a slight bow (see page 20). ⬇

8 Cover the lips with a tissue and brush over the top with translucent powder. ↩

PRO TIP

This make-up is subtle. Although make-up was becoming more accepted in the 1890s, it was still not common to admit to using it. The make-up used here should be applied lightly and blended well to enhance the features.

America's sweetheart

YOU WILL NEED

- Rosy cream blusher
- Brown eyebrow powder
- Beige eyeshadow
- Smoky medium-brown or grey-brown eyeshadow
- Flesh or white eyeliner
- Medium rose pink lipliner
- Vaseline

1 Prepare skin and apply a light, luminous base. Conceal where necessary (see page 16). Apply a rosy cream blusher on the apples of the cheeks for a softer finish. Dab the blusher onto the apple and blend away with a clean finger. Use a light dusting of translucent powder to set the foundation. ⬆

2 Fill in the eyebrows using a brown powder, applying in short strokes from the inner corner, and working outwards with a slanted eyebrow brush. They should be quite thick, and heavier than the modern brow, but neat and tidy. They should not be particularly arched – make them flat/squarish. ⬅

4 Blend the eyeshadow a little at a time around the lash line, up to the socket but no higher than the crease. ⬆

3 Create soft, innocent doe eyes by first applying a beige shadow all over the eye from the lash line to the eyebrow. Follow this with a smoky medium-brown or grey-brown eyeshadow, applied on the outer half of the eyelid only. ⬆

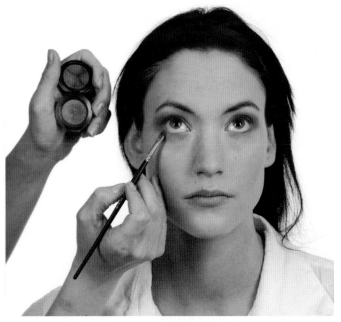

5 Blend the eyeshadow slightly under the eye – use the majority of the product on the outer corners to make the eyes look as big as possible. Ask the model to open her eyes to check the effect and make sure the application is even. ➔

6 Line inside the lower eyelid with flesh or white eyeliner, again to enlarge the eyes. Curl the eyelashes to open as much as possible and apply mascara. ⬇

7 Outline the lips with a lipliner in a medium rose pink, creating an exaggerated rosebud on the top lip. ⬇

8 Fill in the lips with a lip pencil and use Vaseline and a small brush to work it into the lips for a stained look with a definite shape. The Vaseline will give the lips a slightly sheer look. ⬅

PRO TIP

If you don't have a cream blusher, try using a lipstick instead.

Jazz-age flapper

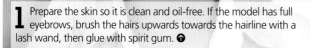

1 Prepare the skin so it is clean and oil-free. If the model has full eyebrows, brush the hairs upwards towards the hairline with a lash wand, then glue with spirit gum. ⬆

2 Block out the eyebrows by applying a thin layer of mortician's wax, working the wax between fingers until it is really soft, then press into the brow outwards and upwards in the direction of the hair growth. ⬆

3 Seal with cosmetic sealer, and blend pale foundation over the whole eye. ⬇

4 Press powder over the concealer to set the make-up. Apply nude beige eyeshadow over the whole eye area. ⬆

5 Mark on the new eyebrows first using a slanted eyebrow bush. They should be higher than the natural brows, with an exaggerated arch. ⬇

6 Draw in the eyebrows using a sharp brow pencil, ensuring the lines are symmetrical. Start by drawing a dot at the inner corner, one at the top of the arch and the outer end, then join the dots. ⬆

7 Line around the whole eye with a black kohl pencil (do one eye from start to finish, then the other eye) corner to corner, top and bottom. Gently lift the eyelid by pushing the brow upwards – this enables you to draw the eyeline at the root of the lashes. ⬇

8 Smudge matt black eyeshadow into the eyeliner, and use a clean brush to blend the edges. Curl the lashes and apply two coats of mascara top and bottom. Choose a pale ivory shade of foundation and apply using a foundation brush to ensure an even coverage. ⬆

11 Fill in the lips with blood-red lipstick, applied with a lip brush. Blot and repeat. Add a touch of clear gloss to the centre of the lips. ⊝

9 Shade under the cheekbones and the sides of the nose with a skin-coloured blusher, slightly darker than the natural skin tone, using a fan brush for the sides of the nose and the flat side of a blusher brush under the cheekbones. ⬆

10 Using a natural-toned lipliner, trace the desired lipline. This should have a pronounced bow in the middle. When you are happy with the lipliner, go over it in red. ⬆

PRO TIP

Begin the look with the eyes as this is heavy eyeshadow that may fall on the skin and would spoil the base.

Jazz-age socialite

YOU WILL NEED

- Brow powder
- Black kohl pencil
- Black eyeshadow
- Grey eyeshadow
- Pressed white eyeshadow
- Black mascara
- Rose pink blusher
- Natural lipliner
- Rich pink lipstick

1 Working on the eyes first, blend some foundation as an eye base over the whole eye area; set with loose powder. Groom the eyebrows, and enhance the brow with natural powder and a small angled brush. Keep the strokes short and work outwards from the nose, keeping the brows thin and neat. ➊

2 Blend a natural colour over the whole eye area from the lashes to the eyebrow. Line along the upper lash line from the inner corner to the outer, using a soft black kohl pencil. Smudge the eyeline and intensify by blending black eyeshadow over the top of the pencil. Blend the outside edge of the black eye colour towards the socket, using a circular movement. ➌

3 Soften the eyeshadow by blending a soft grey eyeshadow around the top of the colour already applied. ➋

5 Highlight under the eyebrow with a white pressed eyeshadow. Curl the eyelashes and apply two coats of mascara to the top lashes and one coat to the bottom lashes. ⬇

4 Using a soft black kohl pencil, take the eyeliner along the inside of the bottom lid, stopping halfway. Soften under the eye by blending black eyeshadow alongside the eyeliner under the bottom lashes. ⬆

6 Clean up any fallen eyeshadow powder. Blend foundation over the rest of the face and set with loose powder; conceal where necessary. Enhance contours of the cheeks with a natural blusher, applied under the cheekbones, then add a rose pink on the cheekbones. ➡

7 Outline the lips with a natural lip pencil to define the shape, and then apply a rich pink colour lipstick over whole lip and blot for a matt finish. ⬆

PRO TIP

For a younger, bolder look, simply
work heavier eyeliner around the eyes.

1930s depression

YOU WILL NEED

- Red greasepaint
- Crepe hair, finely chopped
- Grey-blue aquapaint
- Wig lace (optional)
- Stubble wax
- Stage dirt

1 Prepare the skin to ensure it is clean. Apply a very thin wash of base all over the face (either a cream cake base or a water-based cake using a damp sponge. Work down the neck). Do not conceal. Use a red greasepaint (or if you don't have it use a matt red lipstick) to add a little colour to the apples of the cheeks, forehead and bridge of the nose (all the places the sun would redden). Apply with a small synthetic detail brush (or lip brush) and then blend in with your index finger using a tapping motion rather than stroking. Prepare some hair to enhance the beard line by very finely chopping some prepared crepe hair into a dish. ➊

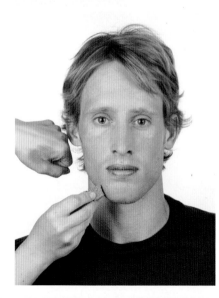

2 Darken the beard line with grey-blue aquapaint applied with a damp stipple sponge. Add a little at a time, lightly touching the sponge to the skin. The effect should not need blending. ➌

3 Ensure the beard line has dried and press loose powder in with a velour puff. Apply a thin layer of stubble wax – warm it up between your fingers so it is really soft and won't upset the make-up underneath. ⬅

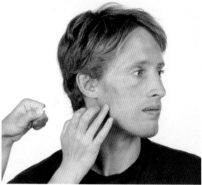

4 Use a light touch when applying the wax and don't drag across the skin. ⬆

5 If you have it available, hold some wig lace against the skin. Dip a large powder brush into the chopped hair, shake off any excess, and then press the head of the brush straight into the wax on the beard line (through the lace if you're using it). The hairs should lie with just the tips in the wax, mimicking the way they would naturally grow. ➡

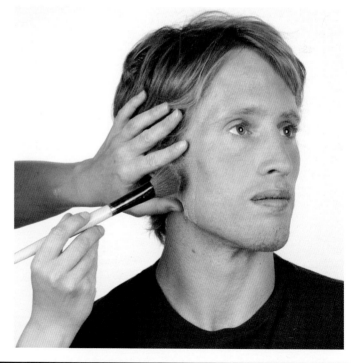

6 Add a little stage dirt, applying at your discretion. The character may have been working on machinery and therefore would have dirty hands which he might have wiped across his face, or he could have picked up a layer of dust which would have collected around the nostrils and over his cheeks and forehead. ⊖

PRO TIP

Stippling on chopped crepe hair for stubble is a good use for crepe hair which would usually be discarded when preparing hair to make a beard or moustache.

1930s Hollywood starlet

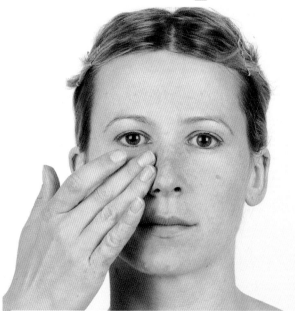

YOU WILL NEED

- Pearly blue eyeshadow
- Lilac eyeshadow
- Individual false eyelash bunches
- Dusky rose cream blusher
- Red lipstick

1 Cleanse the skin and apply a base all over the face, including the eyelids. Conceal where necessary. ⬆

2 Powder to set, using translucent powder. Roll the powder onto the skin using a velour puff, then dust away the excess with a powder brush. ➡

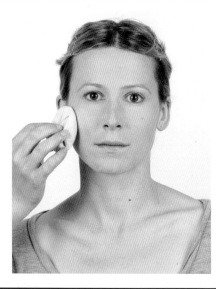

3 Apply a dark-toned contouring blusher beneath the cheekbones. ⬆

4 Use a pearly blue eyeshadow to highlight the eyelids. ⬆

5 Enhance the socket line with lilac eyeshadow. Apply the eyeshadow using a large eyeshadow brush, and blend well. ➡

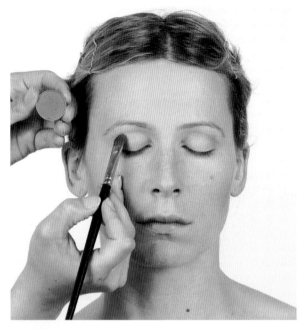

6 Apply some sections of false eyelashes (see page 22). ⬅

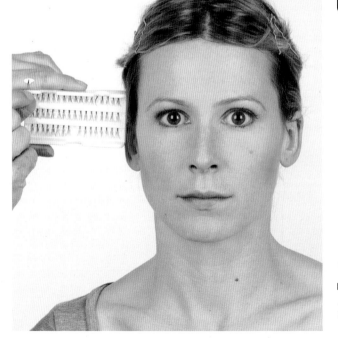

7 Focus the length of the added lashes on the outside of the upper lids. Apply mascara. ⬆

8 Enhance the shape of the eyebrows using a sharpened brown eyebrow pencil. Work from the inner edge of the brow outwards, drawing with the pencil in short strokes, to mimic hairs. ⊙

9 Apply a dusky rose cream blusher from the apples, working the colour back towards the ears. ⊙

10 Line the lips so they look full, with a pronounced bow (see page 20). ⊙

11 Fill in the lip area with lipstick, blot and repeat. ⊙

PRO TIP

When using a lipliner pencil, use a powder puff to support your hand against the skin, and steady the pencil.

1930s leading man

YOU WILL NEED

- Matt cream bronzer
- Matt peachy blusher
- Eyebrow pencil in two shades

1 Following the straight make-up for men routine (see page 18), use a wash of cake make-up over the whole face, including the eyes, and conceal where necessary. Look for redness around the eyes and nostrils. ➊

2 Add a matt cream bronzer on the high points of the face (cheeks, bridge of nose, forehead) and then powder to set. If you have a powder blusher, powder first and then lightly dust with the bronzer. Ensure the bronzer is matt and contains no shimmer. ➋

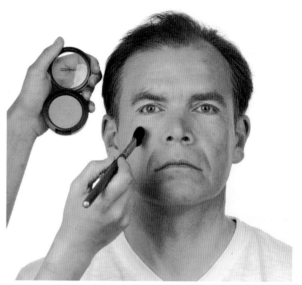

3 Add a small highlight to the high point of the eyelid to open the eye up. Use base or a small amount of concealer in a shade paler than that of the base. ⬆

4 Apply a small amount of a matt peachy blusher on either side of the nose in an upside down triangular shape. ⬆

6 Fill in darker hairs sporadically with a darker pencil. ⬇

5 The moustache is small and neat as an alternative to laying on a crepe hair moustache. Draw it on with an eyebrow pencil. Starting with a light pencil, draw small hairs by making downward strokes with the pencil, starting in the middle and working towards the outside. ⬆

PRO TIP

Leading men were clean shaven with healthy, smooth skin, and small neat moustaches.

WWII forces' sweetheart

YOU WILL NEED

- Nude beige eyeshadow
- Dark brown eyebrow pencil
- Matt, muted pale grey eyeshadow
- Rosy blusher
- False eyelashes
- Matt white eyeshadow

1 Prepare the skin; apply a matt base of normal to heavy coverage, and conceal where necessary. Dust with powder to set. Roll on with a puff until the powder disappears into the skin. ➲

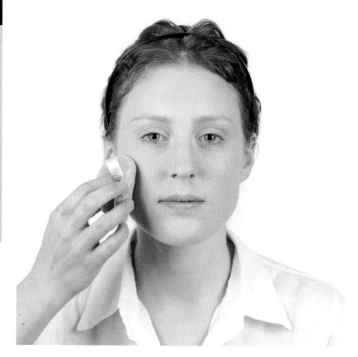

2 Prepare the eye area, using foundation all over the lid up to the brow. Apply a nude beige eyeshadow over the whole lid, highlighting under the arch of the brow with a matt white eyeshadow. ➲

3 Enhance the eyebrows using a dark brown pencil and working in small strokes. ➲

4 Using a matt, muted pale grey, apply eyeshadow from the lash line over the whole lid, up to the socket line. Blend the shadow up towards the brow on the outer half of the eye only. Blend well to soften the edges. ⬆

5 Using liquid eyeliner, draw a line along the top lashes, as close to the root of the lashes as you can get. To help you to reach right to the roots of the lashes, lift the top lid gently by placing your thumb under the brow. Under the eyes should be left clean. ⬆

6 Curl eyelashes and apply mascara to top and bottom (this blends into the false eyelashes better). Apply a full set of false eyelashes (see page 22). ⬅

7 Apply a rosy powder blusher slightly beneath the cheekbone. ⬇

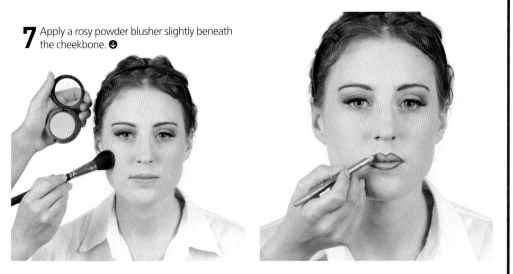

8 Draw in the lipline slightly outside the lips using a pencil lipliner (line first with nude so that it is easier to correct if you make a mistake). Fill in with lip pencil to create a lip base. Coat with a red lipstick (use one with a pinky, rather than an orangey base), blot, and apply lipgloss. ⬆

PRO TIP

When applying blusher, do so after powdering if you are using a powdered blusher, and before powdering if using a cream blusher so that the powder helps it to set.

1940s glamour

YOU WILL NEED

- ● Nude matt eyeshadow
- ● Dark brown matt eyeshadow
- ● Black kohl pencil or a pot of kohl liner
- ● Individual false eyelashes (see page 22)
- ● Pink blusher
- ● Scarlet lipliner
- ● Scarlet lipstick

1 Prepare the skin with a luminizing underbase or primer. Prepare the eye area by applying foundation, followed by a nude matt eyeshadow then a matt white eyeshadow, under the brow bone. ●

3 Blend a very dark matt brown eyeshadow into the kohl line, softening it towards the socket. ●

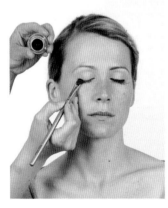

2 Draw along the top lash line with black kohl. Leave the bottom lashes clean. ●

4 Curl the lashes and apply one coat of mascara to the top and bottom. ●

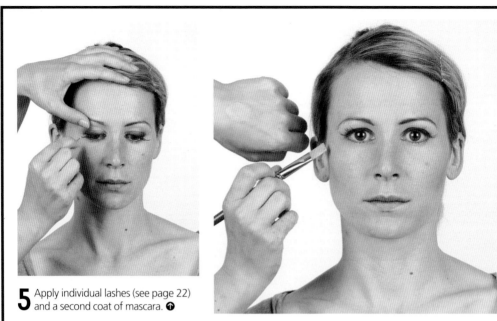

5 Apply individual lashes (see page 22) and a second coat of mascara. ↑

6 Clean up any fallen eyeshadow. Apply a foundation using a matt product with a heavy consistency, or a pan stick in a warm shade. Conceal where necessary. Shade and highlight to improve the facial structure (see page 17). ↑

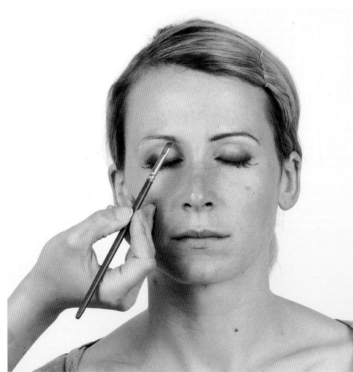

7 Define the eyebrows with eyebrow powder. They should be thin and neat. Using a slanted eyebrow brush, start at the inner corner, making short strokes towards the outer edge. ←

8 Apply pink blusher in a triangle under the cheekbones. ⬇

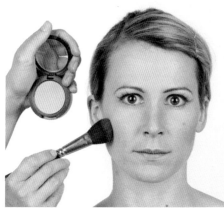

9 Lips in the 1940s were often coloured scarlet-red, in a bowed shape, and slightly overdrawn. Recreate this shape and colour using a scarlet lipliner, then fill in with lipstick (see page 20). ⬆

PRO TIP

A quick way to thin the eyebrows is to use concealer to block out the hairs.

1950s housewife

YOU WILL NEED

- Brown eyeshadow
- Matt beige eyeshadow
- Dark brown eyeshadow
- White pencil eyeliner
- Pink blusher
- Pink lipstick

1 Prepare skin, cleanse, moisturise and apply a base (see page 17). Conceal where necessary (see page 16), and set by dusting with loose powder. ⬆

2 Apply eyeshadow all over the eye area in a matt, beige colour, using a dome blending brush. ⬆

3 Use a taupe eyeshadow to enhance the socket line. Apply into the crease and blend upwards. ⬅

4 Use a dark brown eyeshadow powder and a flat eyeliner brush to line along the top of the eyelids, close to the lash line. ⬇

5 Use brown brow powder to enhance the eyebrows. ⬆

6 Line inside the eyes using a white pencil eyeliner – this is to make them appear bigger. ⬇

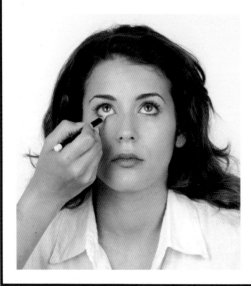

7 Use a contouring colour under the cheekbones (see page 17). ⬆

8 Use a pink blusher on the apples of the cheeks, applied using a circular wrist motion. ➔

9 Line the natural lip shape with a lipliner, and fill in with a pink lipstick. ⬇

PRO TIP

For a natural finish, apply foundation first and then top up the cover where required with concealer.

Blonde bombshell

YOU WILL NEED

- Bronzing powder
- Liquid eyeliner
- Lipstick
- Nude cream or powder eyeshadow
- Matt white eyeshadow
- Taupe eyeshadow
- Brow powder

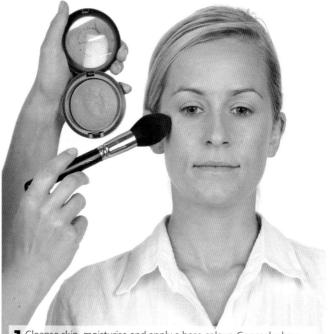

1 Cleanse skin, moisturise and apply a base colour. Conceal where necessary. Add a natural glow to the skin on the high points where the sun would naturally add colour. ⬆

2 Apply either a powder or cream base over the whole eye area. Highlight under the arch of the eyebrow, on the inner corner of the eye, using a matt white eyeshadow. Add definition to the socket by blending taupe eyeshadow into the crease. ⬆

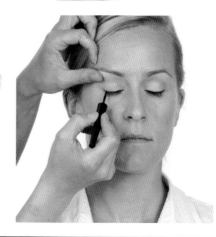

3 Line the eyes along the top lash line with a liquid eyeliner. As you do this, lift the eyelid to pull it taut using the thumb of your other hand. ⬅

4 Curl the eyelashes and apply mascara. ⬇

5 Shade as necessary (see page 17) to improve the facial structure. ⬇

6 Work brow powder through the eyebrows to define them, using a detail brush. Use small strokes and work from the inside of each brow outwards. ⬆

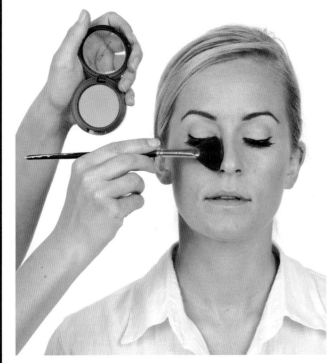

7 Apply blusher to the apples of the cheeks using a circular motion of the wrist. ⬆

9 Line the lips with a natural shade of lip pencil, and apply lipstick in an orangey-red colour (see page 20). ⬆

8 Highlight using a highlighting powder, lightly brushing down the centre of the nose. Powder to set using a luminous dusting powder. ⬆

PRO TIP

Ask your model to smile while you apply the blusher on top of the cheekbones.

YOU WILL NEED

- Eyebrow pencil
- Liquid eyeliner
- Grey eyeshadow
- White powder
- False eyelashes (half)
- Coral blusher
- Coral lipstick
- Clear lipgloss

1950s glamour

1 Apply a base (see page 17). For this look the base should be slightly pale. Shade and highlight the face as required (see page 17). Set with loose translucent powder. Apply the powder with a velour puff, rolling it onto the skin and dusting away with a large powder brush. ⊙

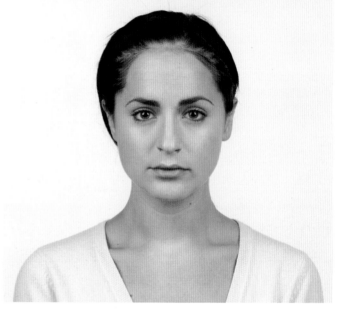

2 The eyebrows should be high and rounded. Create this appearance using an eyebrow pencil. The half closest to the centre of the face is heavier, with the pencil thinning towards the outer edge. Lean your hand against the model's face to keep it steady, resting on a velour puff that will protect the make-up. If the model's eyebrows are not naturally arched, use concealer to create the correct shape. ⊙

3 The 1950s eye look is doe-eyed, with the top lash line slightly extended in a flick. Prepare the eye area first by applying either a cream or powder from the lash line to the eyebrow. Use liquid eyeliner, flicking up slightly at the outer corner. ⊙

4 Use a grey eyeshadow over the lid, from the eyeline you have drawn, to the socket and slightly above. ⬆

5 To emphasize the doe-eyed look, shade with a white powder under the flick of the eyeline. There is no emphasis of the lower eyelid. ➡

6 Curl the eyelashes and apply mascara to the top lashes only. Ask the model to look down and lift the brow with your other hand so that you can reach to the roots of the lashes. ⬇

7 Half-lashes are used from the centre of the lid to the outer corner. Put glue on the back of your hand and run the lashes through it, making sure that there is glue on either end. Place the false lashes on the centre of the eyes and gently push the ends into place. As with the mascara, ask the model to look down and lift the brow so that you can reach the edges of the eye. ⬆

8 Use a subtle coral-toned blusher on the high point of the cheekbone. ⬆

9 In the 1950s, the reds used on the lips in previous periods gave way to softer tones of pink and coral. Line the lips in a coral or natural shade, and apply lipstick. Give the lips shine with a small amount of gloss. ⬆

10 Use liquid eyeliner to draw on a beauty spot halfway between the lash line and the cheekbone. ⬅

PRO TIP

If you don't have a set of half eyelashes, cut a full set in half.

Rock 'n' roll

YOU WILL NEED

- White eyeshadow
- Natural-toned blusher
- Tail comb
- Sectioning clip
- Spirit gum
- Crepe hair
- Hair scissors

1 Cleanse skin and apply a base (see page 18). Conceal where necessary. ➲

2 Use a white eyeshadow to highlight the centre of the eyelids and make the eyes appear more open. ➲

3 Shade and highlight, and apply a light blusher to the apples of the cheeks for some added colour. ➲

4 Use the end of a tail comb to lift the hair out of the way above the ears and clip with a sectioning clip. ➲

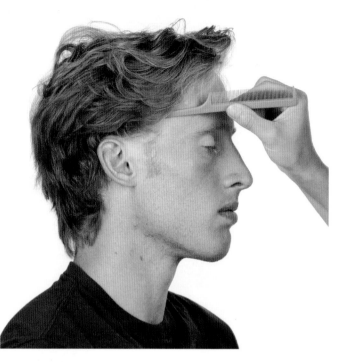

5 Apply some spirit gum to the sideburn area and prepare crepe hair for laying (see page 24). Match the crepe hair to the model's own hair colour. ⬇

6 Glue the crepe hair in stages, starting at the bottom of the sideburn. Press in place with the end of the tail comb. ⬆

7 Continue laying the crepe hair in rows until you reach the join with the hair. ⬇

8 Trim the sideburns vertically to thin and tidy. ↩

PRO TIP

Guyliner didn't come in until the Glam Rock movement of the 1970s, but this movement was brewing throughout the 1950s and 1960s. This look is typical of the period – bronzed and groomed, with longish hair and sideburns to frame the face. For a later 1960s look, which is certainly less mainstream but was popular with some groups, spice this look up with some glitter on the cheeks and strong eye colours.

1960s chick

YOU WILL NEED

- Pale matt pink or white eyeshadow
- Matt black or dark grey eyeshadow
- Beige blusher
- Frosted pink lipstick
- False eyelashes
- Mascara
- Kohl eyeliner

1 Prepare skin. Starting with the eyes, use a nude base all over (cream eye colour or foundation). Press pale matt pink (or white) eyeshadow onto the inner half of the eyelid and over the high point. ➊

2 Start to build the socket, adding a little at a time, using a matt black or very dark grey. Shade the outer half of the lid, along the socket and slightly onto the upper part of the lid for a theatrical effect. ➊

3 Lift the outer corner of the shading upwards so that when the eye is open, it gives a slightly flicked effect. Alternatively, once shading is finished, clean away with a cotton bud at the corner of the eye to give a flicked effect. ➋

4 With a kohl pencil, line along the top lashes, close to the lash line and inside the lower eye. Blend well to soften all hard edges. Groom the brows and lightly fill in if necessary – they should not be heavy. ➡

5 Curl lashes and add a thin coat of mascara. Apply a full set of lashes on top (see page 22). ⬇

6 Apply a second coat of mascara lightly to the false and real lashes, to emphasize and combine together. ⬆

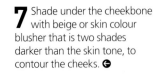

7 Shade under the cheekbone with beige or skin colour blusher that is two shades darker than the skin tone, to contour the cheeks. ⬅

8 Apply frosted pink lipstick – no need for lipliner. Powder lightly to set. ⬇

PRO TIP

The eyes were the focal point of the 1960s face. Great, long, heavily mascaraed eyelashes were often supplemented with false lashes. Eyeshadows in greys, blues, greens and browns, with a dark crease, were in vogue. Eyeliner was dark, usually black and thick. Lips were more subtle, as demonstrated here.

YOU WILL NEED

- Bronzer
- Brown kohl pencil or gel pot
- Light brown, shimmery eyeshadow
- Brown-toned blusher
- Nude or peachy lipgloss

1970s disco

1 Prepare skin and apply luminous under-base for a healthy, glowing finish. ⬇

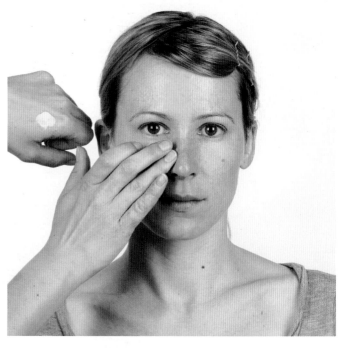

3 Lightly powder with translucent powder using a big brush so that the make-up is set and the T-zone is not shiny, but the face is not obviously powdered. ➜

2 Apply base (see page 17), adding a liquid bronzer to the foundation – choose a foundation that matches the model's own skin tone but is light and luminous. Adding the bronzer will give a healthy glow. Conceal where necessary – lighten dark shadows and hide blemishes – particularly around the nose. ⬆

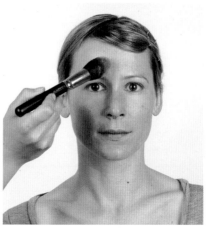

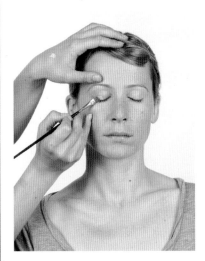

4 Apply a cream eye base in a nude tone all over the eye, from the lashes to the brow. ⬆

5 Line around the eyes with brown kohl using either a gel pot or a pencil underneath and close to the lower lash line. Smudge along the top, bearing in mind that the lines should not meet. ⬆

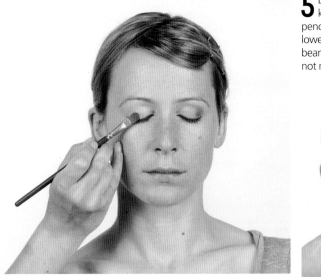

6 Apply a light brown, shimmery eyeshadow on the top eyelid, from the lash line to the socket and slightly higher than the socket on the outside edge. Use a darker brown eyeshadow for more intensity on the outer half. ⬆

7 Curl lashes and apply mascara to top and bottom, making sure there are no smudges. ⬆

8 Apply a brown-toned blusher under the cheekbones to contour, and a peachy tone on the apples of the cheeks for a healthy, fresh look. ⊙

9 Apply a light, natural lip pencil all over the lips in a natural shape (this is a good base for glossy products) and apply gloss in a nude/peachy tone. ⊙

PRO TIP

Eyebrows should be groomed but natural – 1970s women had thin brows. Achieve this look by keeping the wand vertical and moving the hand sideways.

1980s power dressing

YOU WILL NEED

- → Tinted moisturiser
- → Deep pink eyeshadow
- → Pale pink eyeshadow
- → Shimmery, pale nude eyeshadow
- → Dark brown kohl pencil or gel eyeliner
- → Brow powder
- → Strong red blusher
- → Cerise pink lip pencil
- → Tinted lipgloss

1 Prepare the skin. Apply tinted moisturiser over the whole eye area and set with a nude beige eyeshadow. Darken the eye socket with a deep pink eyeshadow and apply a paler pink over the eyelid from the lashes to the socket crease, and on the outer corner above the socket. ⊕

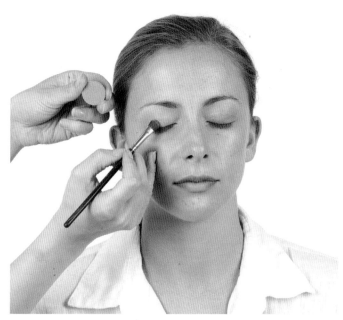

2 Highlight under the brow and in the inner corner of the eye with a shimmery pale nude eyeshadow. ⬆

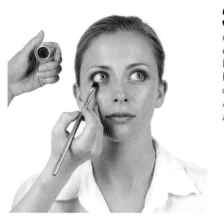

3 Line along the top and bottom lashes with dark brown kohl or a gel eyeliner. On the bottom lashes, work along only half the eye, from the outer corner to the centre. Apply mascara to the top and bottom lashes. ➡

4 Fill in the eyebrows with brow powder, keeping to the model's natural brow shape (don't exaggerate the arch of the brow). Clean up around the eye area and apply tinted moisturiser to the face. Conceal where necessary and set with powder. ⬆

5 Apply blusher with a large blusher brush over the top of the cheekbones and up to the temple. ⬆

6 Line the lips and fill in with a cerise pink lip pencil. Steady the model's chin with your free hand when lining the lips. Add a tinted lipgloss on top of the lip pencil, in a similar shade. ⬅

PRO TIP

The blusher used for this look is a strong red so add a little at a time and build it up.

1980s men's fashion

YOU WILL NEED

- ➔ Shine-control moisturiser
- ➔ Matt bronzer

1 Clean the skin with a wipe or toner on a cotton pad. Avoid using cotton wool on stubble as it will catch. ➔

2 Apply a shine-control moisturiser to make the skin matt.

3 Apply a thin layer of sheer base all over with a sponge. This gives a wash of colour to even out skin tone, but should not be visible. Start in the centre of the face, on the nose. Make sure the colour you use matches the model's skin tone exactly, unless the model is very pale or grey-looking. If necessary, add a second layer of base on the beard line to cover any shadow or stubble. ➔

4 Conceal shadows around the nose, dark patches under the eyes, blemishes and any heavy beard line on the top lip and chin. ⬇

5 If the model has dry lips, apply a thin layer of non-shiny lip balm using a lip brush. ⬆

6 If necessary, very lightly dust a matt bronzer over the high points of the face, starting with a minimum amount and adding more if required. ⬇

7 Powder the T-zone and along the hairline. For a TV studio or stage, press in firmly with a puff; for photographic work, a film, or an outdoor shoot, dust the powder on with a brush. ⬆

PRO TIP

If the man has good skin, do not apply
a base, just conceal dark shadows.
Instead of matt bronzer, you could use
pressed powder in a dark shade.

1980s girls' fashion

YOU WILL NEED

- Taupe eyeshadow
- Brow powder
- Black kohl eyeliner pencil
- Beige blusher
- Deep red lip pencil
- Lipstick

1 Apply a base (see page 17) using a matt foundation over the face. Conceal as necessary, and set with powder. Prepare the eye area with a skin-coloured matt powder, working all over from the lash to brow. ⬇

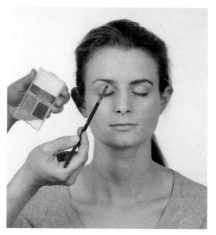

3 Fill in the brows with a brow powder suited to the model's hair colour. Use a slanted brush and fill with short strokes from the inner corner to the outer point. ⬅

2 Blend a light taupe into the socket to create a sense of depth. ⬆

4 Use a soft kohl black eyeliner right around the edge of the eye, along the top of the lash line and on the inside of the lower lid. Ask the model to look to the side so you can reach the inner corner. Work the eye pencil towards the nose then back towards the ear, to reach inside all the creases. ⬇

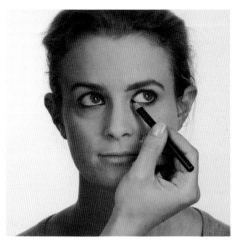

5 Smudge the kohl by blending a matt black powder over the top of the upper line and under the lower lashes. Blend away the edges to soften them slightly, working the brush in both directions. ⬆

6 Curl the eyelashes and apply two coats of mascara (see page 23) on both upper and lower lashes to give a slightly clumpy appearance. ⬇

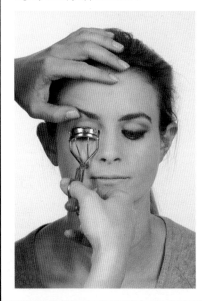

7 Apply a warm beige blusher to a blusher brush. Place the brush flat against the face just under the cheekbone and sweep it backwards towards the top of the ear. ⬆

8 Line the lips with a deep red lip pencil, following the natural shape of the model's own lips (see page 20). ⊙

9 Fill in the lip colour with a lipstick of the same deep red shade. ⊙

PRO TIP

The brows should be full and slightly bushy. Thicken them with powder if necessary.

YOU WILL NEED

- Foundation brush
- Skin-toned eye base or cream eye colour
- Matt white eyeshadow
- Matt pressed powder
- Taupe matt eyeshadow
- Dark brown eyeshadow powder
- Soft pink lipliner
- Soft pink lipstick

1990s glamour

1 Apply a luminizing base and medium-weight foundation (see page 17). Conceal where necessary (see page 16). ➔

3 Lift the eyelid by placing your thumb in the brow to get the product into all the creases. ⬇

2 Prepare the eye area with a skin-toned eye base or cream eye colour, working over the whole eye area from the lash line to the eyebrow. ⬆

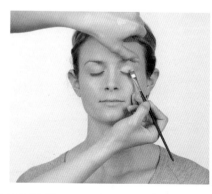

4 Using a matt white eyeshadow, highlight on the browbone, under the arch of the eyebrow, and on the centre of the eyelid. ⬆

5 Groom the eyebrows with a lash wand. Using a slanted eyebrow brush, fill in the brow with a matt pressed powder suitable for the hair colour, making small, short strokes. Start on the inner edge and extend the stroke to a sweep from the middle to the outer point of the brow. ⊙

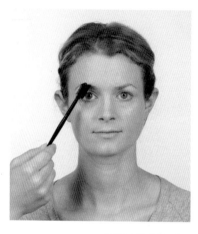

6 Use a taupe matt eyeshadow in the socket line. Ask the model to open her eye and mark slightly on the upper area of the eye, above the part covered by the eyelid. With the model's eye closed, fill down into the socket with the taupe shadow from the line you drew when the eye was open. ⊙

7 Use a domed blending brush to soften the edges of the eyeshadow – there should be no hard lines. ⊙

8 Use a thin liner brush and line along the top lashes, just above the root of the lash, with a dark brown powder. Lift the eye with your other hand on the brow so you get to the roots of the lashes. Blend up from the lash line towards the socket with an eyeshadow brush, making circular movements. ⊙

9 Ask the model to look up and, with the eye detail brush, apply a dark-brown eyeshadow very close to the lower lash line. Work from the outside edges to the centre of the eye. ◖

10 Curl the eyelashes and apply mascara (see page 23) to the upper lashes only. ➔

11 With a soft pink lipliner, trace the outline of the lips, starting with the bow. Then draw from the outer edges towards the centre, repeat on the bottom lip and fill. ⬆

PRO TIP

Using an eye base will mean the make-up lasts for longer – important if the model is to be on set all day.

YOU WILL NEED

- ➲ Pearl beige eyeshadow powder
- ➲ Frosted brown eyeshadow
- ➲ Pink or rose-coloured blusher
- ➲ Sheer red lipstick

1990s grunge

1 Prepare the skin. The base is pale and natural, so choose an ivory-toned tinted moisturiser to even out skin tone. Conceal with a yellow base concealer to cover any imperfections and shadows. Lightly dust with a pressed powder to set the base layer. ⬇

3 Using an eyeshadow brush, press a pearly beige powder eyeshadow over the eyelid.

4 Using a small domed brush, fill the eye crease down to the outer corner, and over the outer half of the eyelid, with a frost-brown colour. Blend the powder as you work it in by making small circular movements with the brush. ⮌

2 Prepare the eye area with a cream eye base in a nude shade applied from lash line to eyebrow. ⬆

5 The eyeliner is the prominent eye product here and is applied fairly thickly, but should appear slightly ragged and rough, as if slept in. Use a dark brown pencil sharpened to a fine point to line around the whole eye from corner to corner, on top and bottom. ➔

6 Using a detail brush, work over the eyeliner on the top of the eyes with the frosted brown eyeshadow which you used in the crease. Brush over the whole eye area with a clean blending brush to blend all the eye make-up together. ⬇

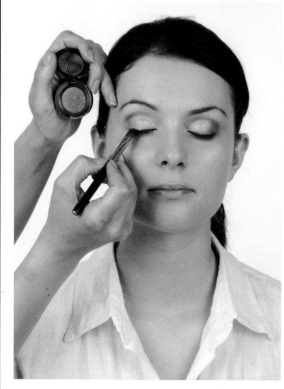

7 Using a medium round brush, apply a soft pink or rose-coloured blusher to the apples of the cheeks. To keep the look soft and natural, also lightly apply blusher to the temples. Dust the whole face with loose powder to blend blusher and base. Curl the eyelashes and apply two coats of mascara to the top lashes, and one coat to the bottom. Separate the lashes with a lash comb. ⬆

8 Fill in the eyebrows using a slanted eyebrow brush and a matt eyeshadow in the same shade as the hair. Make small, short strokes with the brush, working from the inside corner outwards. ➔

9 Line the lips with a natural pink pencil and fill in. Using a lip brush, work a sheer red lipstick or tinted lip balm into the lips. ⬇

PRO TIP

Applying the balm or lipstick with a brush ensures a more even and longer-lasting application.

Bollywood

YOU WILL NEED

- ➔ Beige eyeshadow
- ➔ Matt white eyeshadow
- ➔ Blue liquid eyeliner
- ➔ Peacock blue eyeshadow
- ➔ Grey powder eyeshadow
- ➔ Eyelash glue
- ➔ Bindi
- ➔ Rose-coloured lip pencil
- ➔ Lipgloss
- ➔ False eyelashes

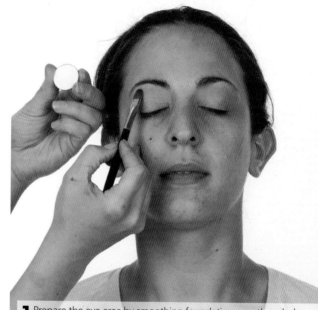

1 Prepare the eye area by smoothing foundation over the whole eye as a neutral base. Then press powder into the base to set. Press beige shadow over the lid using an eyeshadow brush followed by matt white eyeshadow under the brow in the arch. ➔

2 Using a blue liquid eyeliner, draw a line along the top lashes, thinly on the inside and getting thicker towards the outer corner. ⬆

3 Quickly smudge a peacock blue powder eyeshadow into the eyeliner. The eyeliner will bring out the pigment of the powder product. ➔

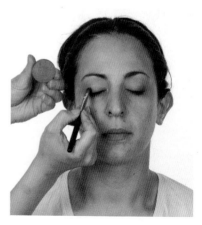

4 Define the eye socket with a grey powder eyshadow. Take only a little powder at a time on your brush to stop it dropping onto the eyelid or cheeks. Tap the brush on the back of your hand first to shake away any excess. ⬇

5 Line all the way around the eye close to the upper and lower lashes using a soft kohl black eye pencil. ⬆

6 Using a detail brush, gently lift the lower lashes and run a thin line of the peacock blue eyeshadow underneath the black line. ⬇

7 When doing a strong eye, build the look up gradually as it is easier to apply more than to take away. Take a step away from the actor/model and assess the impact of the look, and if necessary add more shadow to make it more smoky. Balance the heavily made-up eyes with well-defined, strong brows. First groom the eyebrows using a brow comb or lash wand to brush them into shape. Fill any gaps and strengthen the shape by applying a matt brown eyeshadow or brow powder with an angled brow brush, using short, feathery strokes. ⬆

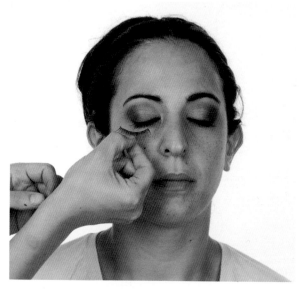

8 Ask the model to look at the floor and curl the eyelashes with eyelash curlers. While the model is still looking down, apply mascara to the top lashes. Ask the model to look forwards and apply mascara to the bottom lashes. Hold false eyelashes against the eye using tweezers to make sure they are not longer than the width of the eyelid. Trim if necessary. Squeeze a thin line of eyelash adhesive along the seam of the false lashes and wait for it to go tacky. With the lashes still held with the tweezers, move them into position and press into the roots of the natural lashes. ⬆

9 Clean away any fallen eye colour from around the eye and then apply the base. Conceal where necessary and dust over loose powder. Using a warm contour tone blusher and blusher brush, apply blusher to the cheekbones. Using a highlighting powder, pale matt beige or white eyeshadow, highlight on top of the cheekbone and down the centre of the nose. ➔

10 Line the lips with a natural, rose-coloured lip pencil, starting with the bow in the centre and going right into the corners, and then fill in completely with the lip pencil. Apply either a tinted gloss in a similar shade or a clear gloss on top. ⬇

11 Use eyelash glue to secure the bindi, placing it a few centimetres above the centre of the brows. ⬅

PRO TIP

Do the eyes first (these colours are strong and may need cleaning up). Once the eyebrows have been groomed into shape, to maintain the shape spritz hairspray on to your brow brush or finger and stroke it across the brow.

CREDITS

All photographs are by Martin Norris, © Quintet Publishing unless otherwise stated below.

Quintet Publishing wishes to thank The Kobal Collection for its picture research, and for permission to use the photographs for the Gallery section of this book.

The Kobal Collection owes its existence to the vision, courage, talent and energy of the men and women who created the movie industry and whose legacies live on through the films they made, the studios they built, and the publicity photographs they took. The Kobal Collection collects, preserves, organises and makes these photographs available.

Kobal and Quintet Publishing wish to thank all the film distribution and production companies listed below, whose publicity stills appear in this book. The publishers apologise in advance for any omissions, and would be pleased to make any necessary changes to future editions.

A = above, *B* = below, *L* = left, *R* = right, *C* = centre, *T* = top, *F* = far

Shutterstock:

P1, P2, P7, P10–13, P28.

Kobal Collection:

P2: *B-C-L* Scott Free/Enigma/Paramount, *B-C-R* Paramount; P3: *L* Universal, *C-L* Jersey Films/Redin, Van, *C-R* Ikiru Films Sl/Dreamworks Skg, *R* 20th Century Fox/Paramount/Wallace, Merie W.; P4: *T* Icon Ent/Buena Vista, *A-F* New Line/James, David, *A* Warner Bros, *C* Hurrell, George, *B* Turner/New Line, *F-B* 20th Century Fox/Powolny, Frank, *B* Universal; P26 Studio Canal/Working Title// Sparham, Laurie; P27: *FL* Tri Star, *L* Touchstone/Universal, *C* Warner Bros, *FR* Warner Bros TV/Bright/ Kauffman/Crane Pro/The Kobal Collection/Jones, Sam; P28 Rasa Film/Ndf International; P29: *A-T* Universal, *A-L* Universal, *A-C* Enigma/Goldcrest/ BSB/Appleby, David, *A-R* ICC/Cine-Trail, *B-T* 20th Century Fox, *B-C* Warner Bros, *B-R* 20th Century Fox; P30: *A-T* Warner Bros/ Bailey, Alex, *A-L* Warner Bros, *A-C* MGM, *A-R* Warner Bros/Bailey, Alex, *B-T* 20th Century Fox, *B-L* MGM, *B-C* Dreamworks/ Universal/Buitendijk, Jaap, *B-R* Dreamworks/ Universal/Buitendijk, Jaap; P31: *A-T* Icon Ent/Buena Vista, *A-L* Icon Ent/Buena Vista, *A-C* Icon Ent/Buena Vista/Cooper, Andrew, *A-R* Icon Ent/Buena Vista, *B-T* 20th Century Fox, *B-L* United Artists, *B-C* Kinofabrika/X-Filme, *B-R* Beijing Film Studio; P32: *A-T* Icon/Ladd Co/ Paramount/Blanshard, Richard N., *A-L* Icon/Ladd Co/Paramount, *A-C* Icon/ Ladd Co/Paramount, *A-R* Icon/Ladd Co/Paramount, *B-T* Sony Pictures Classics/Braun, Steve, *B-L* Paramount, *B-C* Premiere Heure/Schlemmer/France 3; P33: *A-T* HCC Happy Crew Company, *A-L* Anglo - EMI, *A-C* BBC Films/ Focus Features/Bailey, Alex, *A-R* International Film Production, *B-T* Miramax Films/Universal Pictures/Sparham, Laurie, *B-L* Studio Canal/Working Title/Sparham, Laurie, *B-C* Studio Canal/Working Title/Sparham, Laurie, *B-R* Studio Canal/Working Title/Williams, Greg; P34: *A-T* British and Dominions, *A-L* Columbia/Irving Allen, *A-C* Paramount, *A-R* 20th Century Fox, *B-T* Columbia, *B-L* Fox Films, *B-C* Orion/Paramount, *B-R* Ch4/Hal/Portobello/ Daniel, Liam; P35: *A-T* Ikiru Films SL/Dreamworks SKG, *A-L* Warner Bros, *A-C* P.E.A, *A-R* Merchant Ivory, *B-T* Bespoke Films, *B-L* Touchstone/Buena Vista Pictures, *B-C* Warner Bros, *B-R* Hanway/Medusa/RPC; P36: *A-T* Focus Features/ UIP, *A-L* United Artists, *A-C* Working Title, *A-R* MGM, *B-T* Icon/Warner Bros/Hamshere, Keith, *B-L* Paramount, *B-C* Paramount, *B-R* MGM; P37: *A-T* Hook Prods/ Amblin, *A-L* Walt Disney/ Mountain, Peter, *A-C* Walt Disney; *A-R* 20th Century Fox, *B-T* Warner Bros, *B-L* Columbia, *B-C* RKO/Bachrach, Ernest, *B-R* Stanley Kramer/ United Artists; P38: *A-T* 20th Century Fox, *A-L* Imagine/Touchstone, *A-C* Goldwyn/United Artists, *A-R* 20th Century Fox, *B-T* SGF/Gaumont, *B-L* Scott Free/Enigma/

Paramount, *B-C* United Artists, *B-R* Warner Bros; P39: *A-T* Blufilm/Canal+/Gemini/Madragoa, *A-L* 20th Century Fox/Von Unwerth, Ellen, *A-C* Really Useful Films/Joel Schumacher Prods./Bailey, Alex, *A-R* Blufilm/Canal+/Gemini/Madragoa, *B-T* British Lion, *B-L* Icon/Pathe/Bailey, Alex, *B-C* MGM, *B-R* MGM; P40: *A-T* Romulus/Warwick, *A-L* Dreamworks/Warner Bros/Mountain, Peter, *A-C* CBS, *A-R* Paramount, *B-T* Diamond Films, *B-L* Diamond Films, *B-C* Warner Bros, *B-R* Imperiado/British Lion; P41: *A-T* MGM, *A-L* Turner/New Line, *A-C* Turner/New Line, *A-R* Tri Star, *B-T* Di Novi/Columbia, *B-L* Selznick/MGM, *B-C* Selznick/MGM, *B-R* Miramax; P42 *A-T* Miramax, *A-L* Mosfilm, *A-C* Columbia, *A-R* MGM, *B-T* 20th Century Fox, *B-L* Universal, *B-C* 20th Century Fox, *B-R* Orion; P43: *A-T* Columbia Pictures/Dreamworks/Spyglass/James, David, *A-L* Paramount/Dyar, Otto, *A-C* Columbia/Michaels, Darren, *A-R* Paramount, *B-T* Associated British, *B-L* 20th Century Fox/Paramount/Wallace, Merie W., *B-C* Walt Disney Pictures, *B-R* Merchant Ivory; P44: *A-T*

Hesser, Edwin Bower, *B-T* Wardour, *B-L* Paramount/Richee, E. R., *B-C* Miramax/James, David, *B-R* United Artists; P45: *A-T* United Artists, *A-L* Merchant Ivory/Lyric, *A-C* Magnolia/Sweetland, *A-R* K. C. Medien/Foreman, Richard, *B-T* United Artists, *B-L* Universal, *B-C* 20th Century Fox, *B-R* Touchstone/Universal; P46: *A-T* MGM/Hurrell, George, *A-C* United Artists, *A-R* MGM/Bull, Clarence Sinclair, *B-L* Hurrell, George; P47: *A-T* Gainsborough, *A-R* MGM, *B-L* Universal, *B-R* Columbia/Coburn, Bob; P48: *A-C* CBS-TV, *A-R* Warner Bros, *B-R* 20th Century Fox; P49: *A-T* 20th Century Fox/Powolny, Frank, *A-L* MGM, *A-C* Paramount, *A-R* Warner Bros, *B-T* MGM, *B-C* Paramount; P50: *A-T* Warner Bros, *A-L* New Line/James, David, *A-C* MGM, *A-R* United Artists, *B-L* Spelling-Goldberg/Costa, Tony, *B-C* Warner Bros, *B-R* ABC; P51: *A-T* 20th Century Fox, *A-C* Gladden Entertainment, *A-R* Columbia Pictures/Embassy Pictures, *B-T* Baywatch Co/Tower 12 Prods, *B-L* Costa, Tony, *B-C* Paramount, *B-R* Paramount; P52: *A-T* Universal, *A-L* Orion, *A-C* Touchstone, *A-R* MGM,

B-T Warner Bros, *B-L* Warner Bros TV/Bright/Kauffman/Crane Pro/Jones, Sam, *B-C* Anarchy Prods/D'Alema, Guy, *B-R* Fox/Uchitel, Diego; P53: *A-T* Morgan Creek/Davis Films, *A-L* Columbia TV, *A-C* Jersey Films/Redin, Van, *A-R* 20th Century Fox, *B-T* Rasa Film/NDF International, *B-L* Mirabai Films/Delhi Dot Com, *B-C* Pathe Pictures Ltd, *B-R* Fox Searchlight Pictures/Genser, Abbot; P55: Universal; P63: Warner Bros; P67: MGM; P71: Icon Ent/Buena Vista; P75: United Artists; P79: Icon/Ladd Co/Paramount; P83: Premiere Heure/Schlemmer/France 3; P87: Anglo-EMI; P91: Studio Canal/Working Title/Sparham, Laurie; P95: Columbia/Irving Allen; P99: Fox Films; P103: Warner Bros; P107: Touchstone/Buena Vista Pictures; P111: United Artists; P115: Paramount; P119: Walt Disney/Mountain, Peter; P123: Columbia; P127: Imagine/Touchstone; P131: Scott Free/Enigma/Paramount; P135: 20th Century Fox/Von Unwerth, Ellen; P139: Icon/Pathe/Bailey, Alex; P143: Dreamworks/Warner Bros/ Mountain Peter; P147: Diamond Films; P151: Turner/New Line; P155: Selznick/

MGM; P159: Mosfilm; P163: Universal; P167: Paramount/Dyar, Otto; P171: 20th Century Fox/Paramount/Wallace, Merie W.: P179: Paramount/Richee, E.R.; P183: Merchant Ivory/Lyric; P187: Universal; P195: Hurrell, George; P203: Universal; P215: MGM; P223: New Line/James, David; P227: Spelling-Goldberg/Costa, Tony; P235: Costa, Tony; P239: Orion; P243: Warner Bros TV/Bright/Kauffman/Crane Pro/Jones, Sam; P247: Jersey Films/Redin, Van; P251: Mirabai Films/Delhi Dot Com.

INDEX